The Princess Principle

The Princess Principle

Women Helping Women
Discover Their Royal Spirit

Jana L. High and Marilyn Sprague-Smith, M.Ed.

-with-

Lorri Allen ❀ *Sue Bergstrom, M.Ed.* ❀ *Julie D. Burch* ❀ *Jennifer Curtet*

Deb Gauldin, RN ❀ *Sheryl Rudd Kuhn, MRR* ❀ *Carolyn L. Larkin*

Janet Luongo, M.S.Ed. ❀ *Joyce C. Mills, Ph.D.* ❀ *Rebecca Pace* ❀ *Lori Palm* ❀ *Vickie Pokaluk*

Valerie A. Rawls ❀ *Sheryl Roush* ❀ *Sue Stanek, Ph.D.* ❀ *Amy S. Tolbert, Ph.D.*

R & W Publishers
Dallas, TX

If you wish to order additional copies of *The Princess Principle*, please contact:

Rawdon & Watson Publishing Company
5930-E Royal Lane, PMB #221
Dallas, Texas 75230
Toll Free Phone: (866) 820-6303

You may also order online at: *www.princessprinciple.com*

Volume discounts are available.

Published by

Rawdon & Watson Publishing Company
5930-E Royal Lane, PMB #221
Dallas, Texas 75230
Toll Free Phone: (866) 820-6303

Publisher's Cataloging-in-Publication Data
High, Jana L.
    The princess principle : women helping women discover their royal spirit / by Jana L. High and Marilyn Sprague-Smith. — Dallas, TX : Rawdon & Watson, 2003.

        p. ; cm.
    ISBN 0-9714933-1-6

    1. Self-realization. 2. Success. 3. Self-actualization (Psychology) I. Sprague-Smith, Marilyn. II. Title.

BF637.S8 H54   2003   2002093881
158.1   —dc21   0301

"Princess Principle" logo designed by Sandy Tysseland of Plano Type & Graphics

Cover design by Barbara Hodge

Interior design by Debbie Sidman

Project Coordination by Jenkins Group, Inc. • www.bookpublishing.com

Printed in the United States of America

06 05 04 03 02 • 5 4 3 2 1

Contents

Foreword:
The Birth of
the Princess Principle

By Jana L. High

I live an espresso kind of life. It seems that I go from one speaking engagement, meeting, and project to another without enjoying the moment. I can't seem to avoid stress, and just when I think I have things organized and under control, something else pops up.

However, one thing I have decided to take time to do as often as possible is to have lunch with two of my best friends and original princesses, Caryl Cherry and Sandy Tysseland. Between the three of us, we have discovered many common bonds, have shared tons of laughter and tears, and have formed an everlasting friendship.

But let me start at the beginning. During one of my first lunches with Caryl I was complaining about my weight, my looks, my age, my failures, etc. She was doing the same, and suddenly I said, "No, Caryl! This isn't going to work! We are *both* beautiful, intelligent, fun, and we are royal! Yes, we are princesses!" She beamed and readily agreed. We decided right then and there that we were going to call ourselves "The Princess Pal Lunch Group." We immediately put our heads together to decide who else we felt "worthy" to join our exclusive group. I pulled out a pen and paper and started taking notes.

We laughed so hard that, instead of feeling depressed, we found a new bond of appreciation for our royal spirits. Our first order of business was to invite Sandy Tysseland, who is definitely royal and made the first threesome perfect, to join us.

Caryl, Sandy, and I have been enjoying our majestic lunches ever since. We always try to work in shopping (of course) after we eat and talk. We have formed a relationship that is very unique. We don't have to be together all of the time, talk every day, or know every little thing about each other, but we all know that we will always be there for each other.

We were sitting at our favorite meeting place one day when the brainstorm hit to write this book. I said, "Hey, do you remember that business book that was written in the 1970s, *The Peter Principle*? It was a book about corporate America and was written by a man, for men in the workplace." When they both said they did, I told them, "I am going to write a book called *The Princess Principle*. It is going to be a book for women. I want it to be a book of encouragement, challenge, and triumph." My fellow princesses loved the idea and said, "Jana, you must do it!" I wrote the name on a napkin and put it into my purse so that I could develop this idea after I finished my current book project, *High-Tech Etiquette*.

That idea stayed with me and kept creeping up every time I turned around. I would meet women in my seminars, in church, the grocery line, on the elevator (oh, yes, I talk to everyone!) and they all needed encouragement and reassurance of their royal spirit.

Many months later, I was greeting attendees to the National Speakers Association Western Winter Workshop in Honolulu, Hawaii, when a former acquaintance stopped by to register. We had met at a previous speaker's convention and we immediately started "bonding" again. Fact is, we talked for well over an hour before her husband could convince her to leave. We just laughed and talked and as my daughter said, "It was hard to tell when Marilyn stopped and Mom started!" This was the beginning of the best part of the workshop. Along with our husbands, we sat at the same tables for lunches and dinners during the convention. On the last night we were going to be in Hawaii, we went to dinner at a Japanese restaurant. After we ordered, I was talking to Marilyn as we shared our common love for our favorite island, Kauai, when she started talking about her granddaughter being a "princess" and doing the "princess wave."

I said, "Oh, that is so funny! I have to tell you about this group of women who are my princess pals." I shared with her my idea of writing a book called *The Princess Principle*.

Marilyn just stopped dead in her tracks! Her eyes got as big as saucers and she told me that this idea was fabulous. I told her about the direction that I wanted to follow and she and I went crazy sharing ideas. You couldn't separate us. Our poor husbands just looked on and knew they weren't "king for a night"! My daughter Julie, who is also a professional speaker, was with us and was bored to tears. But nothing could stop the synergy that was flowing between Marilyn and me.

It was obvious to me that God had placed us there, at that moment, together. And that is when I asked her to partner with me in this project. Thus, *The Princess Principle* was born!

We have spent hours working out the details of this beautiful project, and it is our hope that you, our readers, will receive the reward. The reward is that each one of you will find a story that will touch your heart, inspire you, and offer encouragement. We are eighteen messengers of hope and faith who have found our royal spirits and want you to find yours.

With that, I cannot possibly thank all of the people who have contributed to this project enough. But I must thank my wonderful Prince Lee, who once again has worked side by side with me on this project and who is my shining knight, truly my "happily ever after"!

It is with gratitude that I also thank each princess who contributed her story to this book to make it a reality.

I also want to thank my precious princess daughters, Julie and Lorie, who continue to remind me of what truly is worthy in life.

It is with this spirit that I hope you enjoy this book and the many more to come.

—Jana High

❧ ❧ ❧

Introduction

By Marilyn Sprague-Smith, M.Ed., CLL

Some things you just *know* are right. There's no logic, no theory, no proof, yet you feel a compelling urge to go forward. So it is with *The Princess Principle*.

This book is the first in a series focusing on women who want to develop their personal and professional lives. Written by everyday heroines, each chapter contains a true personal story of inspiration, of hope, of overcoming life's challenges, and the discovery that our greatest potential is within ourselves.

Why *The Princess Principle*? "Princess" connotes being a member of a royal family, and a "principle" operates at all times, in all situations. Therefore, "the Princess Principle" means you have a *royal* birthright—the Royal Spirit within. It is *always* present and at work in *all* situations.

When we shared *The Princess Principle* definition and vision with colleagues, family, and friends, the overwhelming response was

"Count me in" or "Here's a woman you must contact, she's so-o-o perfect for *The Princess Principle*." Our 18 co-authors are as diverse in their backgrounds as the geographic locations where they reside. From the East Coast to the West Coast, and from the North to the South, these like-spirited women embraced *The Princess Principle* vision to become messengers of hope and inspiration.

In these true stories, you will discover how our everyday heroines allowed their Royal Spirit to function as:

- an inspiration station (just going there makes things go better right now)
- an "any" key (as in "to continue, hit any key")
- a guidance center (where you connect to the most and the best)
- a magic mentor (when you need to be put in touch with a miracle)

Explore the truths contained in these stories and discover that you, too, *can do* whatever you want or need to do because you have a Royal Spirit and you *are* a princess!

Yours in helping women discover their Royal Spirit,
Marilyn Sprague-Smith, M.Ed., CLL

❧ ❧ ❧

Lorri Allen

*B*roadcast journalist Lorri Allen has interviewed more than two thousand people, and one day she realized that some people seem happier than others, even in the face of despair. She also observed that some were intimidated by the TV camera, despite an important message to share. Didn't everybody deserve a little good news? Didn't everyone deserve a chance to articulate a meaningful message? That was the beginning of Lorri's company, *Good News!* Not only does Lorri work with people who want to increase their media effectiveness, she also presents positive, upbeat messages designed to encourage and inspire.

Lorri holds a degree in journalism from The University of Texas at Austin. She is also an author and professional speaker. Her affiliations include the National Speakers Association, the Radio and TV News Directors Association, and the NSA-North Texas chapter.

Lorri began speaking when she was asked to join her junior high school's speech tournament team. A consistent winner, she achieved the prestigious ranking of Double Ruby with the NFL— the National Forensic League!

On a personal note, Lorri is happily married to Mark, who besides being a brilliant photographer, editor, producer, and husband, is also an award-winning filmmaker.

Lorri can be contacted at: Lorri Allen
Allen, Texas
Good News!
toll free: (888) 785-3466
www.Lorri.com

Pretty as a Princess? Royalty Begins on the Inside

By Lorri Allen

We all have princess potential. But for some of us, the trials and troubles of life crowd in and we lose our focus on the kingdom. This is my journey from princess to dungeon dweller and back. I hope it encourages you.

From an early age, I knew I had the royal blood of a beauty queen flowing inside my veins. The story I learned by heart was the one about how my parents met. My mother had won the local Farm Bureau Queen Contest, and when Darrell saw her grinning photo in the newspaper, he fell in love. After a few fairytale twists and turns, they were married eighteen months later.

Problem was, I look more like my dad. And I was often outcast because of my size. You know, the one always picked last for the team. The one who couldn't climb the rope or jump over the high bar. Some people are cursed with a sweet tooth. I got thirty-two of them. Still, I slimmed down enough in high school to enjoy participating in speech tournaments and stage plays. In college, I decided I wanted to be a TV reporter. I didn't think about my looks playing a role in my success. In those days, the role models were Walter Cronkite and Barbara Walters, two journalists blessed with more brains than beauty. The guidance counselor said you had to be able to write and talk. I could do that! And reporters were always traveling around the world. They were at the scenes of chaos and adventure. They were always the first to know current events. It sounded like an exciting job to me.

Since I could write and speak, it came as a surprise when an assignment editor told me as an intern in a television newsroom, "You're no Miss America, so you're going to have to work very hard in this business."

In retrospect, it was the best career advice any twenty-year-old could get. At the time, though, it just hurt my feelings.

A few years—and a few more pounds—later, the same mentor said, "You're never going to make it as a broadcast journalist if you don't lose some weight."

Another year later, having all hopes pinned on a job in a new city, a news director told me, "Well, it came down to you and another young woman. We chose her for obvious cosmetic reasons."

I hung up the phone politely, then collapsed into sobs.

In each of these instances, I wanted to scream what I had always been told, "You can't judge a book by its cover! Beauty is only skin deep! Pretty is as pretty does! I'm a very hard worker! And besides, my mother won the Kleberg County Farm Bureau Queen Contest!"

But I kept silent, more and more convinced that beauty was the coin of the realm and my purse was empty. I was a resident of the dungeon, shackled to the chains of others' opinions.

Despite the blows to my self-esteem, I kept working very hard. The reputation of being diligent helped me land a job in 1989 at the Automotive Satellite Television Network, behind the scenes, as a news producer.

For fun in my spare time, I began to sail and train for marathons. For the first time ever, I felt healthy and alive. Spiritually, I had found a church that challenged and blessed me. I had a new self-esteem that comes from a strong body, good relationships with God and friends, and a steady paycheck. You may not have seen my reports on ABC, CBS, or NBC, but I worked very hard and enjoyed my job. Finally, I walked tall with the confidence of a princess. The best part was, I liked myself and didn't care so much anymore whether news directors thought I had "on air" potential. When I completed that first marathon, no tiara could have been worn more proudly than the medal I earned that marked me as a "finisher."

In 1993, the hard work again paid off when I was promoted to news director. Now it would be my turn to hire people! Oh, I was tempted to seek out refugees like me from other newsrooms. I had succeeded when others predicted I wouldn't make it. So, maybe I could give other journalists a second chance. I knew I would be willing to overlook a few extra pounds, a few wrinkles, a crooked nose, a little gray hair. Broadcasting might be a looks-driven business, but brains still mattered. The ability to sniff out a story, write compelling copy, and stack an interesting, accurate newscast were just as important in our newsroom, if not more, than a pretty face.

My life was happy, but I wondered if there would ever be a Prince Charming in my castle. I loved being single, but every once in a while the palace got a little lonely. I thought it would be terrific to have someone special in my life to share all of the happiness. But I had turned thirty, and it seemed like all the nice princes had already found kingdoms to run. So I resigned myself to the idea that if Mr. Charming ever made an appearance, he would be a really big dream come true.

One day, a photographer from another department asked if he could go jogging with me. I agreed, and afterward he asked, "Are you really happy doing what you do? You are so pretty that you could be anything or do anything you want to."

Me, pretty? No one had used that word to describe me in a long time. Like since my grandmother had uttered it when I was six. He said it so sincerely that I was taken aback. I wanted to believe him. But just the fact that *he* thought I was pretty was enough to make me feel like Cinderella at the ball.

The sweet, handsome photographer and I started jogging together more often. He continued to say all of the right things and, as fairytales go, we fell in love. Soon, I married this Prince Charming who made me feel like royalty.

A few years … a few pounds … and more wrinkles later … he still does and says all of the right things to help me believe that I am beautiful. And in our real-life fairytale, I know that we will live happily ever after.

It's kind of funny, but now that I don't seem to care that I have no coins of the realm, people are often telling me how good I look. They may just be trying to be nice. Some people even comment on how much I resemble my mother! I am not saying at age forty that I am ready to win a beauty pageant. No, far from it. I am saying that I feel as pretty as a princess, from the inside out.

When I finally realized that I really was a princess, I wanted to share the formula with other women. The principle is really pretty simple. You don't have to run a marathon. Not everyone can do that. You don't have to fall in love. Plenty of princesses never meet a Prince Charming. You don't even have to land an exciting job where you hire people or lead a department.

The secret to being a princess, feeling like a princess, and knowing that royal blood flows in your veins is not what you wear on your head, but what you have between your ears. Not so much being intelligent, but being smart enough to figure out what will give you self-confidence and going after it. For most of us, that is setting a realistic but difficult goal and seeing it through. For me, that goal was running a marathon and becoming healthy in the process. At one point, running 26.2 miles—in the same day—seemed more impossible than realistic. After all, I was the chubby non-athlete picked last for every team. But here's a huge part of the self-confidence formula: what you were yesterday does not define you today. Each day brings a clean slate of possibilities and opportunities to excel and be a more perfect princess than you were the day before.

Your realistic but difficult goal may be getting a raise, starting your own company, writing a book, or purchasing your own home. Whatever will make you feel good about yourself, decide right now, once and for all, that you are going to take a step toward that goal each day.

Putting off your goal with excuses or busy-ness is keeping you from feeling great about yourself, and that is a terrible return on the investment of your future.

You may think princesses sit on satin chaise lounges and eat chocolate all day, but the princesses I know work very hard. It may seem ironic, but the harder I work, the faster and sweeter the fairytales occur.

So, I encourage you to work hard to reach your goal to increase your self-confidence. Believe in the best future you can imagine. Picture it, taste it, feel it. Imagine your castle. See yourself polishing your tiara.

Dreams do come true. Even really big ones.

I am fortunate. I'm the daughter of a Farm Bureau beauty queen and a child of the Heavenly King, married to Prince Charming. I can't help but be a princess.

❧ ❧ ❧

Sue Bergstrom

Sue Bergstrom brings over sixteen years of strategic human resource management and organization development experience to her organizational consulting role. She has served both profit and not-for-profit organizations, specializing in employee, team, and leadership development and offering guidance and support in implementing local, national, and global human development initiatives.

Sue holds a Master's Degree in Human Resource Development from the University of Minnesota, where she is currently enrolled as a doctoral student. She contributes to the academic, professional, and Christian communities as a first-class teacher, lecturer, and keynote speaker. She makes topics come alive with her honesty, knowledge, and sense of humor, quickly engaging her audiences with the experiences and lessons that she shares.

Sue can be contacted at: Sue Bergstrom
sueb@spacestar.net

Running the Race

By Sue Bergstrom M.Ed.

"**M**y mommy won the Grandma's Marathon race," my four-year-old daughter announced to her friends as she dangled my bronze medallion in front of their faces.

In a way she was right because, for me, *winning* the marathon simply meant *finishing* in under six hours, which I accomplished with an ample five minutes to spare. To be exact, running Grandma's Marathon provided me with five hours, fifty-four minutes, and fifty-three seconds of a personal faith-building experience.

I had trained for six long months for this event. I had run in sub-zero temperatures and bone-chilling wind chills. I had run in sleet and snow. I had run in torrential rains. Occasionally I had the privilege of running with a partner, but mostly I ran alone. Friends who had previously run marathons coached me for this day. "When the going gets tough," they would say, "remember to stay focused on your goal." I visualized myself crossing the finish line (in an upright position) and leaving the city of Duluth proudly displaying my new t-shirt that would simply say, "GRANDMA'S MARATHON: FINISHER."

The race day began on a positive note. While standing in one of the satellite bathroom lines before the race began, I met Amy, a woman who was about to run her second marathon. We chatted just long enough to know that our finishing goals were similar, and we quickly agreed to run the race side-by-side. We continued to talk as we took our places in the starting line-up. I checked my watch. I rubbed my palms together and breathed on them to create warmth. I stretched my hamstrings and checked my watch again. I shuffled from foot to foot. Then, the starting gun fired and Amy and I slowly moved forward within the sea of seven thousand runners.

With Amy as my new running companion, I hardly noticed I was exerting effort. We exchanged information about our families, our jobs, and our lives. An instant bond formed, and my confidence surged as I realized that accomplishing my goal would be much easier with Amy by my side. My newfound confidence, however, was short-lived. Not long after mile three, Amy suddenly dropped out of the race with a severe muscle pull. I reluctantly continued on my journey much like I had trained—alone.

But as I approached the five-mile marker, my eyes lit up and a smile emerged as I spotted my daughter planted securely on my husband's shoulders next to my best friend.

"Go Mommy!" a tiny voice squealed.

My family and best friend enthusiastically cheered me on.

"Would you like some juice? A bite of a banana?" they offered.

Without hesitation, I shook my head and squeezed my daughter's hand, trying not to slow my pace for long. With a huge grin on my face, I waved to my fan club and rejoined the crowd of runners. Finishing the marathon would soon be a pleasant memory, I thought.

Then something happened. Each step I took suddenly sent knives of pain up my calf. The pain was intense by mile six, and I knew the last twenty miles would be incredibly difficult. Certainly there was no turning back now, however. I concentrated on the finish line and the finisher's t-shirt that I would take home.

I tried to appreciate the beauty of the lake, the woods, the sky. But all I could think about was the pain. Step after step. And then I heard it again.

"Go Mommy!" a familiar voice rang out unexpectedly from the sideline.

Could it be? My family and best friend were waiting for me again at mile twelve. I crossed over to their side of the road, swept my daughter into my arms, and gladly accepted the flower she had picked especially for me. I momentarily forgot about the pain.

As I continued on, I silently celebrated passing the 13.1-mile marker. I knew I had half the race behind me, but I also knew I had 13.1 miles to go. I grew more and more discouraged as I began to fall to the back of the pack and lose contact with the company of other runners. I stared at the pavement and concentrated on moving my feet.

Somewhere around mile fourteen, when things were really tough, I looked up and spotted what I thought to be a familiar face on the sideline. Our gazes connected.

The woman inquired, "What are *you* doing here?"

I echoed, "What are *you* doing here?"

My co-worker and I were each unaware that the other would be at the race, but before I knew it, she was running along beside me, encouraging me to keep going and assuring me that she would pray for me to be strong. We laughed and talked and quickly hugged as she hastened me along my way.

In about a quarter of a mile I was on my own again, but my spirits had once again been renewed. Moving my legs seemed a little easier for a couple of miles. But then things became *really* tough—tougher than I had ever known before, even in all my hours of tedious training. I prayed for someone to run beside me, because I knew that I could not finish the race without the companionship of another runner. Within seconds of murmuring that prayer, a woman pulled up from behind.

"Do you mind if I run with you?" she asked.

For the next ten miles, Mimi and I encouraged each other, challenged each other, and held each other accountable. With about twenty miles behind us, we were approaching the infamous Lemon Drop Hill. We literally moaned as we climbed to the top of its crest.

"Are you okay?" I heard Mimi ask.

"I'm okay. Are you okay?"

"I'm okay. We're going to make it!"

"Yes! We're going to make it!"

Six miles doesn't sound like a long way to go, but we felt the impact of every step. Instead of woods and lakes and wildlife, the sights and sounds of the city now surrounded us. As we approached downtown historic Duluth, our feet pounded on the crevices of the cobblestone street. We spotted the balloons announcing only two miles to go. At that point, two miles seemed like eternity.

Finally, I spotted the finish line. An unexpected surge of energy replenished my weary body.

"Mimi, I need to go for it!" I shouted as I shifted my gait from a slow jog to a full stride and sprinted down the final stretch.

I threw my arms in the air in sheer delight and choked back tears as I crossed the finish line. I was greeted on the other side with my commemorative medallion, covered with a thermal cape, and directed to the t-shirt tent where I received the infamous shirt that only finishers receive. The race was over, I had my prize, and now I could rest.

With my first (and last) marathon now six years behind me, I stay focused on running a different kind of race. It's called life. Like my marathon, this race is marked by moments of celebration and victory and ecstatic joy. But it is also laced with moments of despair and great disappointment. One message always remains constant—I desperately need other people to help me stay in the race.

Earlier this year I entered a new turn in my race of life—the loss of my job. For months, everyone on my work team lived in fear as we saw the events of 9/11 profoundly impact the business of our firm. We watched as other groups within our organization experienced layoffs, but we all clung to the hope that our own team would not be affected.

I clearly remember how that dreadful day began. Shortly after arriving at work, my phone rang.

"Hi, this is Sue," I answered.

"Sue, could you come into my office?" my boss asked. She never called me into her office. I knew. I grabbed a handful of tissues and proceeded to her corner of our floor. I passed through her partially opened door to see tears in her eyes.

"This is hard for me," my boss began. I don't remember anything about the meeting after that.

While my first week of unemployment was mostly a blur, what I do remember is receiving e-mails and hand-written notes and phone calls from people who cared. Their encouragement became my strength—strength that I needed to continue on with this race, despite the sadness and shock and fear that threatened my confidence.

As I engaged in my job search, I received yet another blow. While working out at the health club one morning, my left knee suddenly collapsed. A nearby trainer assisted me to a chair, where he examined my swollen knee.

"You need to see a doctor immediately," he advised as he took my arm to help me out of my chair. With one arm on his shoulder, I strained to get to my car without bending the injured knee.

I drove home in silence through six inches of freshly fallen April snow, where I fell into my husband's arms and sobbed relentlessly for the next twenty minutes.

"We'll get through this," he said. Once again, he was there to support me in my race.

On an old pair of borrowed crutches, I hobbled to the office of an orthopedic surgeon. I groaned in pain as the X-ray technician struggled to position me for the X-rays. The surgeon briefly examined me and scheduled me for knee surgery on the first available date, which was five days later. But in just three days, I was facing a final round of interviews with a prominent organization's senior leadership team. Even though any slight movement of my knee literally took my breath away, I proceeded with the interviews.

Upon arrival at their executive offices, I navigated my way to the door on my crutches. I concentrated on my feet, examining the ground for any bumps or crevices that could cause me to stumble.

"What happened to you?" each interviewer asked as we met.

The crutches served as a conversation starter, and I quickly formed bonds with the executives who shared stories of their own past knee injuries. I responded to their interview questions with confidence and absorbed information they shared with me.

"How did it go?" my husband inquired upon my return from the interviews.

"I am so excited about this job opportunity!" I exclaimed. "Everything about it seems right!"

With the interviews complete and my knee immobilized in a steel brace pending surgery, my attention turned to my daughter, who was home sick with the flu. With two days remaining until my surgery, I watched helplessly as she lay tossing and turning on the living room sofa, burning with fever. My husband tirelessly cared for us both.

On the morning of my surgery, I woke to what seemed to be a cruel joke—a sore throat and a fever of my own. The thermometer read 99.5 degrees. I called the hospital and spoke to the anesthesiologist, who said they would proceed with the operation only if my temperature did not get any higher. One thing I knew for sure—I desperately needed the surgery!

A few minutes later, my daughter awoke for the sixth consecutive day with a 101-degree temperature. We struggled to find someone who would be willing to care for a sick child while my husband and I traveled to the hospital for the surgery that I hoped would still occur. We struck out over and over as we contacted the names on our list of friends and relatives. Then, an unexpected call came to me. A colleague who had been laid off with me was phoning to wish me well on my surgery. When she learned of our predicament, she immediately offered to leave her new job to come and stay with our daughter. She wanted to run the race with me.

I took my temperature one last time. It had crept to one hundred degrees. I called a couple of dear friends, who prayed with an extra measure of faith that my temperature would return to normal in time for my surgery. Fifteen minutes later, when we arrived at the hospital, my temperature was normal. The doctors would proceed.

Immediately following my operation, the surgeon met with my husband.

"A piece of cartilage, the size of a dime," she explained to him, "broke off from the groove of her knee joint and was lodged behind her knee cap. I removed the piece of cartilage, but there is a hole in her joint that her kneecap will catch on when she bends her knee. I hope that, in time, the edges will wear down and the knee will be able to bend freely."

She was mildly optimistic.

Two days later, I lay stretched across my bed with my leg elevated on two giant-sized pillows and my knee wrapped in ice packs. Barely coherent from the pain medication, the phone next to my bed startled me when it rang. I fumbled to pick up the receiver and muttered a hoarse hello.

"We'd like to extend you an offer," the voice on the other end of the receiver announced.

I accepted the offer. I couldn't jump up and down with excitement, but I was ecstatic to be offered my ideal job—and the only job I have ever interviewed for on crutches.

I delayed my start date to allow extra time for healing, but the recovery proved long and difficult. Caring friends, who continued to run this race by my side, provided meals, flowers, and countless cards. After six weeks on crutches, I struggled to regain my strength and to take my first step without aid.

"You can do it, Mom!" my daughter cheered. I tested my step before trusting all of my weight on the unpredictable knee.

With a voice now more mature and an understanding now more complete, my daughter once again stood at the sideline to cheer me on. Her words evoked deep emotion as I concentrated on the challenge in front of me. We both knew that this race was even more difficult—and more important—to "win" than the marathon six years earlier.

"Good job, Mom!" she affirmed as the first step led to another, then another.

With the surgery now just a memory, each step continues to lead to another, then another. Today I walked by a woman in a wheelchair parked on a busy sidewalk.

"Could someone please push me to the corner?" I heard a soft voice ask. My friends waited for me while I eagerly assisted the woman to her destination.

"Thank you!" she replied and patted me on my arm.

Indeed, it was my turn to help someone else run her race.

ℰ ℰ ℰ

Julie D. Burch

*J*ulie Burch is an internationally recognized speaker who gets results! She believes in delivering a seminar that is high-energy, loaded with humor, and full of tangible, usable information that is cleverly disguised as fun.

In addition to being an adjunct instructor at Southern Methodist University and an active member of the National Speakers Association, Julie has designed and presented seminars for industry leaders such as the Southwest Corporate Federal Credit Union, the University of Medicine and Dentistry of New Jersey, Emcare, Convatec, Concentra, the American Payroll Association, Tino's Restaurant, Outback Steakhouse, Le Meridien, and the Boys and Girls Club of America.

Julie shares her message of "Take back control" through her popular keynote topics of *Going the Distance* and *Fortunately ... Life's a Cookie*. Her dynamic and captivating presentations will not soon be forgotten. Her audiences leave exhilarated and enlightened!

Julie can be contacted at: Julie D. Burch
JLH Presentations
toll free: (866) 820-6303
Julie@jlhpresentations.com
www.jlhpresentations.com

The Glass Slipper

By Julie D. Burch

I have always loved Cinderella. I wanted to *be* Cinderella. I even looked a little like her. My mom always called me a toe-headed blonde with green eyes. I guess all little girls have their favorite princess, and for as long as I can remember, Cinderella was mine.

I was born and raised in Southern California, so Disneyland was nearby. In fact, Disneyland was a summer staple for my family, as we went every year. My earliest memories of Disneyland didn't revolve around the typical things. It wasn't "It's a Small World," "The Pirates of the Caribbean," or "Space Mountain." For me, Disneyland meant only one very important thing: I got to see Cinderella in the Main Street Electrical Parade.

I remember being about six years old and dragging my family to the parade line-up, long before we really needed to be there, so I could get a front row seat. I waited impatiently, fidgeting all the while, for Cinderella's pumpkin-shaped carriage to bring her around the bend.

All the other Disney characters paraded by, but that was not why I was there. "Hurry! What is taking her soooo long? Where is she?" I would exclaim ad nauseam. My mom would have to calm me down. "She will be here. Be patient." But to a child of six, the minutes seemed like an eternity.

And then there she was, seated regally in her horse-drawn carriage with her prince at her side and wearing the most beautiful gown I had ever seen. I would fall into a quiet daze of amazement. In my mind, Cinderella epitomized everything a woman should be. She was beautiful, graceful, kind, loving, generous, and she never lost her temper. She was a true princess. I wanted to be just like her.

I don't remember ever leaving the park at night. I think I must have floated out on my fantasies, because as soon as I saw Cinderella at Disneyland, I became her in my mind. I could see it so clearly. I was beautiful, graceful, kind, and loving to everyone around me. Then my prince would come and sweep me off my feet. He would take me away from the housework and the chores and the mean people in the world. We would live in a big castle and have big parties where I was the most gracious hostess. We would have lots of children and I would be the perfect mom. We would, in short, live happily ever after.

My dad thought of me as a princess, too. He often treated me like one. I was a very lucky little girl. I grew up with all the advantages. I had a nice home with loving parents and supportive siblings. We actually really got along! I always had the best clothes and the best opportunities. I had the best of everything. I could not have asked for a better childhood. I was never a spoiled brat, because my mom would never have allowed it. Also, in great part, I believed I was

Cinderella. Cinderella would have never been bratty, rude, or talked back to her mother. I was sweet and loving just like her.

As I grew older and became a teenager, my thoughts of being Cinderella remained, mostly in the back of my mind. My dad, however, reminded me on a regular basis that I was indeed a princess. But looking back now, I see that his definition was different than mine. He told me often that I was expensive and "high-maintenance." When I would tell him I wanted to live in Hawaii, what kind of house I wanted, car I wanted, or how I wanted lots of children, he would tell me that I had better marry rich.

I remember one very specific instance when I was thirteen years old. My dad and I were in the kitchen and he was eating Oreos out of the bag. I reached to take one and Dad said to me, "You'd better not eat that. You'll get fat and you still have to find a husband!"

I didn't understand that this was a bad thing. My daddy showed me how much he loved me every day. He always said how proud he was of me. He told me I was beautiful. He told me I was a "charmer" and constantly showed me off to his friends. I was in pageants, plays, cheerleading, and dance. His friends would come over to visit and he would bring me in and introduce me as his daughter and then have me perform a dance or a monologue from one of my pageants. I loved it. I was Daddy's little girl, and he was so proud of me.

I grew up and believed I could charm my prince. After all, I charmed my daddy. I was Daddy's little princess.

I did become quite the charmer, but unfortunately, my dad went away anyway. When I was fourteen years old, my daddy left. I couldn't charm him to stay. We moved to a new city with new people, and I had to start all over. It was difficult at first, but I survived. I learned to charm again.

I grew up and graduated. I then spent the first of many years of my adulthood looking for my prince. I didn't find one. Oh, I found plenty of options. There were men, but none of them seemed to fit the picture in my mind of what my prince was supposed to be like. So, I did the only thing my years of inexperience had taught me. I found one particular man I thought had great potential (famous last words), and I proceeded to try to *change him*. I hadn't learned the lesson that you can't change other people. Like so many others, I tried.

Someone told me one time that *that* is the lesson you learn in your first marriage: you can't change other people. I wish I had known it back then. I convinced myself he was going to be my prince, and I worked to make it happen. I tried to charm him into submission and make him think I was beautiful, graceful, loving, and giving. I tried to show him I would be the best wife he could ever have. I didn't understand why he didn't seem to get it. I was so loving, giving, and generous to him, and he was mean to me. He treated me terribly. He lied, cheated, and broke my heart, and I let him. The relationship lasted three years. They say we all have a breaking point, and I guess three years was mine. I was a lost soul. The only thing I was supposed to do with my life was find a husband, and I had failed.

This was the one thing I was supposed to be good at, and apparently I wasn't. I wasn't a princess. The words "find a husband" and "You'd better marry rich" played over and over in my mind. I became very depressed. I cried all the time, and I stopped eating. Then I got sick. I barely got out of bed for a week. I had no energy and my body ached all over. This was the second time the most important man in my life had left me and I had been unable to stop him. I had tried being loving, gracious, and giving like any good princess, but it had not worked.

Then something happened. It was an instant rush of emotion, but it was different, a type of emotion I had not let out in many years. I got mad. It was very un-princess like, but it was a real, raw emotion that was all mine. I started thinking to myself that I was tired of feeling this way. I was tired of being in bed. I was tired of not working, and rent was coming due. Then my little voice got louder. I started talking to myself out loud. I would have thought I was going crazy, but it felt too good. I was tired of being a victim. I was tired of not being in control of my own feelings and my own emotions. I was tired of letting a man dictate how I felt. As quickly as the emotion came to my mind, it followed to my body. What I was thinking became my reality.

My body started feeling stronger and I sat up in bed. For the first time since he had left, I had energy. I felt strong. I was in my home alone and all of a sudden I jumped out of bed and got loud. I was working myself up into a frenzy of anger. Shaking my fists and waving my arms, I fought back. I yelled at him for what he had done and I yelled at myself for letting him do it. All of a sudden, from out of nowhere, I screamed at the top of my lungs, "*No more!* I will not allow you to control my feelings and my life anymore. I won't let you do this to me. I am better than this. I am more than this. I deserve more than this."

I don't know where it came from, but this was the single strongest moment of my life. It was the moment I *took back control*. I started getting excited. I saw a light at the end of the tunnel. My life was not over. In fact, *my* life was just beginning. I had spent the last three years living my life for someone else, and I had found no happiness or satisfaction in it. Now it was my turn. I would live for me. I was going to be selfish for the sake of my sanity. I thought how that was not very princess-like. Then it dawned on me: this was the most princess-like thought I had ever had in my life.

I had been trying since I was a child to gain the love and adoration of others by convincing them I was beautiful, loving, graceful, giving, and kind—all of the traditional princess qualities. I had been trying so hard to get other people to see it that *I* never had a chance to see it. How did I ever hope to have anyone else see me as beautiful if I did not see myself as beautiful? How would anyone else ever see me as loving if I wasn't even able to love myself? How could I be kind or giving to others if I couldn't be kind and giving to myself? I stopped at this revelation.

I slowly walked to the bathroom and stood in front of the mirror and stared at my reflection. For the first time in my life, I looked into my own eyes and I really saw *me*. I saw a woman who had made a lot of mistakes—a woman who had made a lot of bad choices. I also saw a woman who was beautiful, graceful, loving, giving, and kind. For the first time in my life, I loved her. I started to cry and then I started to laugh, because I knew that from this moment on, it didn't matter if anyone else liked me. I liked me. And it felt good.

This revelation led me to some very serious soul searching. What I discovered was not a new theory by any means, but it was new to me. I had believed my whole life that I was in control and I had relished that belief. It was wrong. I had allowed other people and other entities to determine what and who I was. I had let them dictate what success for me would look like. I had spent my life defining myself by other people's definitions. Society had told me and my dad had reinforced the notion that pretty girls got married. So, if I could find a good husband and "trap" him (like my dad used to say), I was a successful woman. If I could have 2.3 children, a dog, and a beautiful house with a white picket fence, I was a successful woman. Society, through magazines, television, and movies, told me that I should be five foot seven and weigh one hundred and eight pounds and look like Farrah Fawcett, and I would be a successful woman. I had to keep a clean house, vacuum in my best pearls and dress, do all the laundry, cook a gourmet dinner from scratch every night, manage the house, and all the while keep my job to be a successful woman.

I was tired. It was too much. When I finally took the time to ask myself what makes *me* happy … I mean *really* happy … I was startled by my own response.

What I discovered was surprising and very unconventional. I discovered I liked working. I liked being in control and independent. I liked being alone. When I allowed myself to step back and measure my life by *my* standards, I found success. I had to learn to look at things from a different perspective, *my* perspective.

Right now, I don't think I want children or even a husband. I don't want a house with a white picket fence. I definitely don't want to vacuum in a dress, let alone pearls. I am happy being five foot four. Right now I like being single. I want to travel the world and be the wild and crazy favorite aunt to all my nieces and nephews. I want to buy my own castle.

Apparently this notion takes a lot of people by surprise. Generally, when people hear my declaration of independence, they give me a look of pity. Then they pat my forearm and say, "It's okay. Someday you will meet the right man." I just smile. I know that my idea of a successful life is just as foreign to them as theirs is to me. Does this make theirs wrong? No. Does it make mine wrong? No. We are just different.

I still love Cinderella, but for a different reason now. The traits of Cinderella that embody what it means to be a princess haven't changed, but now I know that those traits must come from within.

You must be able to see them when you look in the mirror. You cannot wait to hear them from someone else. You must be you, and you are special.

Now, in my thirties, I have discovered that it doesn't matter which path you choose. Whether you decide to take a more traditional route or a more unconventional one, you are a princess because *you choose it*. You do it on your terms. There is no greater success.

As for me, I have decided that the best way for me to get my prince is to start my own company, become a huge success in my field, and when I need one, I will hire a prince as my assistant!

❧ ❧ ❧

Jennifer Curtet

*J*ennifer Curtet is burning up the highways across the country with her powerful workshops and keynotes. Her energy and passion have won her rave reviews as "the most motivational speaker ever heard—absolutely amazing!" She delivers information-rich seminars packed with real-world, practical skills, tempered with her own mixture of warmth and humor.

As a trainer and manager for Morgan Stanley Dean Witter, Jennifer was responsible for developing and delivering training programs that are still required for all levels of leadership.

Jennifer established her company, Aristocrat Training and Development, through which she delivers keynotes, conferences, and seminars around the world.

A devoted mentor, Jennifer has committed her life to developing excellence in others. She has been a speaker for the Make-A-Wish Foundation and has most recently co-founded a nationwide nonprofit program for teenage girls. Girls Rule™ is an empowerment program designed to build self-esteem, develop communication and leadership skills, encourage safe choices, and create personal success.

Jennifer can be contacted at: Jennifer Curtet
Aristocrat Training and
Development
11037 Meadow Leaf Avenue
Las Vegas, NV 89144
(602) 421-8653
aristocratenterprises.com
jennifer@aristocratenterprises.com

Live, Laugh, and Be She-She

By Jennifer Curtet

As far back as I can remember, I was the princess. I was always the princess. But not quite the version you may think of at first. I was the only girl in a family of many boys. They were typical guys: loud, rambunctious, competitive, and rough. Consequently, that put me at the bottom of the pecking order. Survival was the name of the game, and I was bound and determined to not only survive among them but to thrive.

I had to constantly prove myself to them. This meant I learned to fish, shoot a gun, ride a motorcycle, climb trees, play football, and anything else they deemed worthy. I was willing to do anything to prove I was their equal: I ran faster, hit harder, yelled louder, and tried desperately not to cry when things got tough. I wore the same clothes, cut my hair the same way they did, and went by a nickname that sounded like it could be the name of a boy: Jeffy! I was a tomboy through and through, and I was also one of the guys. I loved that.

Unfortunately, Mom didn't love it as much as I did. She did everything she could to turn me into her version of a princess. Every chance she had, she put my limp, straight hair in pink sponge-curlers and my athletic body in dresses. Satin, silk, and chiffon … bows, ribbons, and flowers. You name it, she tried it—and I hated every bit of it. One year I decided I wanted a Dorothy Hamill haircut, which of course pleased her to no end. She figured this would be cute, perky, and feminine. Finally, she'd make me She-She. Because I was only six, it was decided that a beauty salon would be much too extravagant for a child. So, she took me to a much less costly, and seemingly more appropriate, barber shop. These poor barbers didn't know what we were asking for. In complete confusion they asked, "Whatsa Dorothy Hamill?" As if we were speaking a foreign language! I tried my best to flip my hair around just like she did on the ice rink, jumping through the air, twirling as if I were having my Olympic debut. They didn't get it. Needless to say, I received my first and only bowl cut. Moments after the visit to the barber, a woman walked up, patted me on the top of the head, and said to my mom, "What a handsome little boy you have!" So much for cute, perky, and feminine.

It was a constant battle to make me a princess. I wanted blue; she wanted pink. I wanted soccer; she wanted dance. I wanted denim; she wanted ruffles. On and on it went … until that glorious Saturday afternoon. I was tied up tightly and curled to perfection. My feet were stuffed like sausages into white patent leather shoes. Every hair was in place and I was looking perfectly prissy. We all piled into the green family station wagon to head down to Sears for the annual family picture. As Mom sat in the front seat, talking a mile a minute, I realized this was the opportunity I had been waiting for. I looked around to make sure the coast was clear, then I quietly rolled down the back window, pulled the bow out of my overly coiffed hair, sat up on my knees, and rode the rest of the way with my head hanging out of the car like the happiest dog on the planet. When we parked the car and Mom saw me, it was like the fourth of July—sparks were flying, doors were banging, and Mom was screaming like a Piccolo Pete! But I won my battle.

As the years went by, I remained an active little girl who was in love with life. I was always the most athletic. I was mouthy and competitive, popular and likable. I had lots of friends, both boys and girls. But then adolescence kicked in. Something very strange happens at this time: self-consciousness soars through the roof and, like a bad joke, self-confidence crashes through the floor. Suddenly you become overly critical of everything that is said and done. Your hair isn't right; your clothes aren't right. Your house isn't right; your parents aren't right. Nothing is right. To make it all even worse, the boys—my pals—didn't see me the same way anymore. Suddenly, they didn't think I should be playing their games. I wasn't good enough anymore. I wasn't fast enough anymore. An invisible line had been drawn between us, and I had somehow been left on the wrong side. The boys started chasing the She-She girls, the girls in pink frills and dresses. And, for the first time, I was left out.

I couldn't figure out how things had changed so quickly. In total desperation, I decided there was only one thing to do: be She-She. All the women in my family embodied She-She-ness: elegance, femininity, and panache. They always had the latest styles and enough moxie to fill up a room. They were always in high heels and draped with beautiful jewelry. They had big hair.

I was like a convert to a new religion. I would watch the way they could talk and laugh about anything for hours on end. I took notes and listened intently. I checked everything out, from what was in their closets to what they had in their medicine cabinets. I tried on their jewelry and their lotions—anything to experience their divine femininity.

During one of the journeys into She-She-ness, I found myself investigating the Queendom of She-She: my Grandmother's bathroom. I was overjoyed to find an absolute cornucopia of potions and perfumes on her delicate tray that sat on the counter. I was so excited that I could hardly keep my hands still. How had I missed all of this for so long? There were bottles of lavender, lily of the valley, vanilla, spice, and rose. As I opened them one by one, the scents filled the bathroom and my senses with excitement and wonder. I put everything on. I drenched every last inch of my little body with the heavenly smells. I was on the verge of She-She. As I continued to search for more, I came across a lovely round porcelain box. It looked like it had been made for a princess. Just from the looks of it, I knew that it must certainly hold the most important treasure in the bathroom. Very gently, I opened the box to find soft pink powder. As I looked at it, I thought of every spectacular movie star I had ever watched, putting on luxurious powder with a big white powder puff. That was it, I decided. I needed a puff!

I searched through everything, rifling through medicine and cleansers, brushes and toilet paper. I combed through the closets, the cupboards, and the shelves. Then I found it in the bottom a drawer— a baby blue powder puff. Victory! I ran to the box and lifted the delicate lid, then placed my puff into the soft, fine, rose-colored powder. I covered every bit of it, making sure there was plenty on the puff for my whole body. I ran the puff gingerly over my arms and hands and then up my neck toward my face. I daintily brushed over my jaw line, then my nose and up on my forehead. I put it behind my ears and on the back of my neck, just like the movie stars had always done. I was covered with the magical pink powder, and I had never felt more beautiful. Like any princess would, I threw my shoulders back and walked regally out of the bathroom to show off my newly found femininity. I was boasting about everything I had put on, from the perfumes to the powder.

It all came to a screeching halt when Grandma claimed she didn't have any powder! Feeling like I had discovered the greatest secret on the planet, I grabbed her hand and quickly pulled her into her bathroom to show her the treasure I had found. The moment she recognized the box, she doubled over in laughter and tears streamed down her face. To my horror, I found that I was covered, dreadfully, from head to toe in denture powder. At that moment, I realized that being She-She was much tougher than it appeared.

From that point forward, my grandmother took me under her wing. She knew it would take a lot of work to turn this ugly duckling into a swan. This woman was truly the epitome of She-She. She was stylish and feminine, yet sassy and confident. She was always beautifully done up, from her clothes to her hair to her nails that were manicured to perfection. But what made this woman special—different even—was her incredible love of life, which I have rarely seen in others since. She was gregarious and bold. Her laughter and silliness were unmatched. She could walk into a room and have everyone giggling within minutes. She was selfless and giving, at all costs. From this amazing woman, I learned that being She-She was something much greater than the way you looked: It was a choice in living.

Early on in her young life, her father abandoned the family, forcing her mother to work multiple jobs and endless hours. It was simply too much to handle alone. At age five, my grandmother was placed in an orphanage. She would see her exhausted mother on weekends and would try desperately to ease some of the sorrow and guilt that she felt. During those years, my grandmother's quiet resolve grew. She committed to never again live a neglected and sorrow-filled existence and made a choice to live life to its fullest. She did this gloriously every day.

That is what being She-She is all about. It is strength and confidence. It is purpose and conviction. It is having the drive to create your own masterpiece, even when others feel they have the right to control the painting. We have all been given a blank canvas and, most importantly, we all have been given the use of any color and brush that we choose. Women, for the first time in history, are being given opportunities that were never expected even thirty years ago. Now is the time to regally spread our wings and take flight. We must commit to finding our purpose, whatever it may be, and we need to find joy in every step within that process. We must find the courage to create a life of vibrant fuchsias, electric blues, and brilliant limes. For too long we have deliberated over the right brush, the perfect hue, the best lighting … For too long we have waited for something more, wanted for something that we thought was just out of reach. This is our divine canvas … so paint! We must paint with passion, paint with zest, paint with conviction, paint with our hearts. This is our sacred gift—this is our choice in living.

Recently, my choices seemed to be disappearing. My mother was diagnosed with breast cancer and the colors on my canvas started to fade. I was angry, and hopeless. How could this happen to *my* mother? She was optimistic and healthy, helpful and giving. This couldn't be happening. We were horrified and depressed at the thought of losing her. But somehow, in the midst of suffering, my mother found the determination and grit to beat this unfortunate diagnosis. She found it for herself and, like the true princess that she is, found it for us too. Soon after we received the dreadful news, the family was sitting around the breakfast table eating in silence. We were all drowning in our despair over the possible loss of our mom. But, being the matriarch that she is, my mother decided that she was going to fix this situation. She started to tell us all about the strides that have been made in medicine for victims of breast cancer. She said that when they now do the mastectomy, they are able to start the reconstructive process—the plastic surgery—at the same time so that a woman never has to live looking disfigured. She exuberantly asked, "Isn't that amazing?" and we just looked at her in complete silence.

Not deterred for a moment by our lack of enthusiasm, she went on. She said that there is a brand new procedure in the reconstructive process during which the diseased tissue is replaced by fat collected from the woman's stomach. She looked at us and said, "How cool is that?" Again, no response.

Finally, with one last effort, she pulled out all the stops. She said that after she healed and the scarring had faded, the doctors would have to make sure that aesthetically both sides looked the same, since she was having a single mastectomy. She said that they would take a tattoo gun—a real live tattoo gun—and they would tattoo her body to make sure that the shape and color of the operated side were the same as the shape and color of the natural side. Finally she looked at us and said, "How incredible is that?" and the entire family burst into tears.

Frustrated at our inappropriate response, Mom jumped up out of her chair, slammed her hand on the table, and yelled, "Alright you guys, enough is enough! Dry your tears; this is a bump in the road. As far as I'm concerned, I'm getting a boob-job, a tummy tuck, and a tattoo all in one day. Life doesn't get any better!" And at that moment it hit me: we truly do have a choice in the lives that we create for ourselves.

So, there it is: the secret of She-She. This gift has been passed down through the generations of women in our family and has become our way of living. Our credo. Our mission. And the amazing thing is, I found that I had it all along, even as a tomboy. In fact, what I've found is that being She-She has nothing to do with perfumes, lotions, or denture powder. She-She is a way of being. It's an aura, a glow, a love of life. It is a joy and a presence that radiates from a love of self and love of family. It's a confidence and a determination to find fulfillment. It is a solid first impression and a delightful lasting impression. It is strength and sensitivity, beauty and humility. It's the right word at the perfect moment, the right gift with the perfect sentiment, and can certainly be the right scarf with the perfect suit. It is living life with moxie yet being able to enjoy the gift of well-earned serenity. It is the ability to laugh at life's foibles and persevere through life's worst. It is the gift of being, innately, a princess. And this I have learned from the women in my life: my grandmother, my mother, my family, my teachers, my sisters, and my fellow princesses. For these gifts, I am forever grateful.

Deb Gauldin

*D*eb Gauldin, RN, *PMS*,* is a pro-fessional speaker and enter-tainer specializing in women's well-being and healthcare morale. A long-time champion of women's causes, Deb draws on over twenty years experience as an obstetric nurse and childbirth educator. Accompanying herself on acoustic guitar, she creates a powerful connection with her audiences using original songs, stories, and humor.

Deb is also an author and cartoonist for several national publications. Her CDs and videos of "Hormone Affirming Music and Humor" are used in educational settings in six countries. A nursing caregiver both on and off the platform, Deb also uses therapeutic humor to manage her two teenage children and husband.

Deb can be contacted at: Deb Gauldin Productions
ON251 Robbins
Winfield, IL 60190
toll free: (800) 682-2347
deb@debgauldin.com
www.debgauldin.com

*Premenstrual Syndrome

Beautiful Just as You Are

By Deb Gauldin, RN, PMS

I applied to join the Peace Corps in the fourth grade. In the sixth grade, sporting Go-Go boots and hot orange fishnet stockings that I carefully hid from my mother until I reached the elementary school, I staged a press conference denouncing the war in Vietnam.

Back then, I clearly believed I could and would make a difference. I thought I could change the world. But, like many young women, I found that somewhere along the line self-confidence and a sense of value had been replaced with insecurity and self- doubt.

I grew to believe that only extraordinary people could make extraordinary accomplishments, and I was feeling anything but exceptional. I wasn't as self-sacrificing as Mother Teresa. I wasn't as brave as Amelia Earhart. I wasn't as smart, talented, athletic, and certainly not as beautiful as the princess I aspired to be. Perhaps I wouldn't be the reigning Miss America after all.

Like so many women, I began a quest to become someone, anyone, but me. I learned to say and do whatever would please others. What everyone else thought, especially about me, became what mattered most. Gradually, I lost a sense of who I was and even lost touch with what I believed.

If I could just lose weight. If I could just learn to keep my voice low and my legs together. If I just knew more about current events or could just sew the perfect seasonal craft! Nothing about me felt good enough.

I compensated by overachieving, yet underneath the veneer of this perky nurse, wife, and mother, I felt a deep void. It was a void that no clever craft project, PTA presidency, or carefully coifed, well-behaved children could fill. I figured the God of my childhood had already tallied all my shortcomings. I didn't even feel I measured up enough to attend church. The ache within me grew so large that I turned to bingeing for comfort and purging to appear normal. I became busier and busier, running faster and faster away from anything resembling my true self.

At wit's end and with my eating out of control, I found myself running into the self-help section of our local bookstore. Boy, did I identify with the women in those books. Ravenously, I would read the first three chapters of each book and marvel at how much I related to the problems. But as I got to chapters four, five, and six, where the authors made suggestions for modifying behavior or taking action in order to change, heck, I would lose interest in the book! Off I would run to read the first few chapters of yet another book. I didn't realize it until much later, but for nearly eight years I was actually doing a tutorial on what was wrong with me!

About that time, I received a flier from a local community college describing a class for women called "Journey into Self." This was it! It was close and affordable. I would "find myself" at the local college! Little did I know that this course and the collective wisdom of the three marvelous women who taught it, Jo Ann Wolf, Sharon Brown, and Pat Paulson, would indeed change my life forever.

I remember arriving for that first class, having dutifully prepared dinner for my husband and the kids before I left. I entered the room not knowing a soul and quickly decided I would sit near the back for an easy escape. Though it was a course scheduled to meet for six weeks, I planned to give these instructors three weeks to "find" and fix me. Good luck!

I registered and immediately looked around the room to determine who "my friends" were going to be. Scanning the students, I caught myself making sweeping judgments about the other women enrolled. "She must have had an easy life," I said to myself. "Look at her hair!" I knew nothing about these women, yet I had already labeled them.

One of the first exercises we did was to break into groups according to similar personality traits. I joined the women who considered themselves outgoing, boisterous, and as some would say, loud and obnoxious. We were called the *Alivenesses*. In the center of the room was the largest group of women, identifying themselves as more quiet and introverted, and deeply concerned with issues of fairness and equality. Some would say they were boring. They were called the *Truths*. The remaining few women, the *Workabilities*, were the kind of people who make to-do lists and actually do them! They know where their car keys are! Their socks may be arranged by color gradation in their drawers! The word "anal" comes to mind.

We began to explore what was good about being in our own group, as well as ways we were often misunderstood. We also looked at our attitudes about the other personalities. I was most enamored with the women who were in the Workability group. I longed to be so organized and thorough. As for the Truths, my entire life I had honestly believed that quiet women were simply so much smarter than I that they didn't bother talking to me. There they were, sitting quietly, thinking, thinking, thinking!

"Nothing could be further from the truth," said the Truths! In fact, they found "life of the party" types like me charming and personable. They longed to join in with quick witty comments, but pointed out that Alivenesses *never shut up!* Try as they might, they felt they couldn't get a word in! I had never looked at it that way. Meanwhile, the Workabilities were still neatly recording their comments into alphabetical columns.

At our next session, we were asked to choose a partner, take sack lunches onto the lawn outside the building, and do a short writing assignment. From across the room I spied a woman approaching me. I smiled weakly. She was *not* one of my chosen "would-be-friends." My mind shrieked, "Don't pick me! Don't pick me!" as she continued toward me and softly asked if I wanted to be her partner. I paused. I considered running. "Of course!" I replied enthusiastically.

Once on the lawn, I sat down. I was wearing my usual gauze skirt and sandals, and simply sat down on the grass and began rooting around in my handbag for a pen. I watched as my partner carefully laid her jacket onto the lawn. She methodically smoothed every—single—wrinkle—out of the coat, the collar, and each arm. She was wearing slacks. Her long, slender legs and knees together, she slowly sashayed down upon the coat. She reached into her purse and quickly retrieved a perfectly—I mean perfectly—pointed pencil. The sun was shimmering off her highlighted hair and "ding" went the sparkle on her tooth.

I looked at her and she looked at me. She appeared to be everything I had ever wanted to look like. Then she said something I will never get over. She looked at me intensely and said with complete sincerity, "You know, I would give anything to be 'earthy' like you."

"Earthy?" My world stopped. "Why yes," I responded. "I am earthy all right. That's what they always say about me … earthy, earthy, earthy." I was astounded. Never did it occur to me that anyone would ever want to be anything like me. This lovely, tidy, slim woman wanted to be more like *me*?

Back in the classroom, we shared from our writing assignments. Meditative breathing set to soothing music followed. I might add here that for the rest of the day, I was dropping little tufts of grass and traces of earth. In fact, this class had no idea how literally "earthy" I was! Then the three instructors, each beautifully representing one of the three different personality categories, shared a simple and profound message. I may have heard it before, but this time I heard it with my heart and soul. They declared to each woman in that class, "You are beautiful … just as you are. Right here. Right now."

Again, I was astounded. I remember immediately rejecting the notion. They simply didn't know enough about me. "Get to know me and you will see I am not okay," I thought to myself. On the one hand, I wanted to shove at them a list of my obvious imperfections, get my tuition refunded, and run as fast and as far away as possible. On the other hand, I felt like collapsing into a heap of emotion, overcome with the realization that perhaps I didn't have to try so hard to be somebody I am not.

Could it really be true? Could I, Deb Gauldin, be whole and beautiful and have all I need just as I am? Could I let the world see the real me? Was there a gentle God who wanted me to celebrate what is good about me rather than flog myself day after day over my imperfections?

Something profound shifted in me. I wish I could say that since that very day, I have bounced out of bed loving myself unconditionally, having never again judged another woman. That has not been the case, but I have learned to honor and celebrate the gifts and talents that make me who I am. I have learned that I can strengthen the Truth and Workability aspects of my personality without denying my delightful Aliveness.

I have learned that it isn't my place to judge another woman for her choices. I have learned that, regardless of outside appearances, we are more alike inside than we may think. I have learned that the best way to make a difference in the lives of others is to be myself and that every difference I make is in fact extraordinary. I have learned that I don't have to be Florence Nightingale or Indira Ghandi to make a difference. I don't even have to wear contraband fishnets!

I have learned that I am beautiful just as I am. Just as all of you are beautiful and whole and have all you need right here, right now. Beautiful women coming together can and will indeed change the world. When we acknowledge and honor the royal spirit that is uniquely ours, we do make a difference.

⌁ ⌁ ⌁

Jana L. High

*J*ana High is an author as well as a full-of-energy seminar leader and keynote speaker. Her presentations are delivered with an enthusiastic and dynamic speaking style. Coupled with her ability to teach "usable" techniques for problem solving, Jana simply captivates her audiences.

In addition to serving as an adjunct instructor for Southern Methodist University, Jana has designed and delivered seminars, keynotes, and training programs for major corporations, organizations, and agencies.

As a highly sought after keynote presenter, Jana's presentations are delivered with humor, high energy, and enthusiasm. They will exhilarate and entertain audiences to encourage them to believe they can achieve their greatest dreams.

Jana Makes Your Meetings Memorable!
Keynotes-Motivational Programs
Business-Organization-Agency Seminars

Jana can be contacted at: Jana L. High
JLH Presentations
toll free: (866) 820-6303
jana@jlhpresentations.com
www.jlhpresentations.com

Dolly, Elvis, and Reba!

By Jana L. High

Three famous singers helped me to realize a special spirit inside of me, although at the time I wasn't really aware of how Dolly Parton, Elvis Presley, and Reba McEntire would change my life. But let's start at the beginning …

Dolly

It's really hard to describe the loneliness of being an unwanted child. I know because I was one. My parents made this well known to me in private, while in public they seemed attentive and caring. I don't have many pleasant memories of my childhood. I was born in Indiana and at age ten, we moved to Ogden, Utah. I remember sitting in our living room and looking out at incredible mountains. The mountains had their own special moods as they changed colors through the seasons. Many were the times I wanted to run away and climb to the top of those mountains and blend in so no one could find me and hurt me again.

It wasn't just at home that things were so sad in my life. The kids at school didn't like me either and their parents wouldn't let them play with me because I wasn't a Mormon. I didn't understand this because I went to Sunday School every week—just not at the Mormon church.

Also, I was tall and thin (oh, for those days again!) with long strawberry blond hair. When I was in the seventh grade, I towered over almost all of the boys in my class. I endured being called "string bean," "toothpick legs," "chicken legs" and constantly was told how ugly I was. Since there was no positive reinforcement from home, I believed it. My Dad used to say, "Jan, you're pretty—pretty ugly and pretty apt to stay that way!" My older brother loved the way Mother and Dad teased me, so of course he joined in with cruel teasing as well.

It isn't any wonder that I became self-conscious when I started developing breasts. No one else in my class seemed to have them, but oh my, I did, and they were big! They grew almost overnight and I had no idea what was going on with my body. These were things we just didn't discuss in my house.

One day, a neighbor girl asked me to come over to play. I was so excited as no one had ever wanted to play with the non-Mormon girl before. We went into her bedroom and she pulled out a funny looking white thing with straps and hooks. She said it was a brassiere that her mom had bought for her to wear when she started to "develop," but she wanted me to have it because the kids were making fun of me. Apparently I bounced and jiggled when I walked.

With her help I put it on. This was one of the first kind things that anyone had done for me and I was grateful. I had no idea she was setting me up for disaster.

At home, I went into the kitchen to let my mother know I was back. She looked at me with a strange, critical eye, but suddenly, much to my surprise, she pulled me into her arms! As I savored this special moment, I thought, "She smells like lilacs and her skin is so soft and warm." I could smell the yeast roll dough on her beautiful lavender apron and a wave of hunger passed through me as I could taste her fabulous rolls. My heart was so full in that brief moment as I couldn't remember my mother ever hugging me like this before. My eyes were closed as I prayed that God would always let me feel this special comfort.

But then, I found out why my mother gave me that hug. She had seen the bra beneath my blouse and this was her way of confronting me. She grabbed at my back, found the bra strap, and pulled me around while lifting my blouse. She screamed, "Where did you get this? Did you steal it?"

I fell to the ground and with tears in my eyes I sobbed, "No, I didn't steal it. Carol gave it to me. She told me her mom bought it for her and since all the kids at school were making fun of me, she wanted to help."

My mother ordered me to take it off immediately. I never argued with my mother as I feared the punishment from my dad would be severe, so I followed her orders.

Later that night, my father came into my room and threw a sack on my bed. He said nothing and walked out. Inside the sack were two bras.

The next morning I put one on and went to school. At recess five girls gathered around me, including Carol. They shoved me into a stall in the girl's bathroom and told me to lift my blouse. I was scared and horrified. When I refused, they told me they had been "assigned" to see if I "stuffed my bra." Stuff my bra—why would I? I refused to show them and they starting pushing and hitting me. I fought back, but I was outnumbered. They lifted my blouse and started making fun of me because I was a "freak" of huge proportions. I pushed one of the girls, Linda, into a heater. Her head cracked open and started to bleed. That scared everyone and they ran, leaving me there to cope with my assailant. I wet a paper towel and put it on her head. Just then, two teachers came in and started yelling at me for fighting. I was hauled off to the principal's office, but I was too embarrassed to explain what had happened. At this point, I figured my dad would kill me anyway, so I needn't worry about any lousy school punishment.

Then, to my surprise, Linda came in and told the principal that we were kidding around and she accidentally fell into the heater and that I was just trying to help her.

My humiliation continued as I kept getting bigger and bigger. Boys at school wanted to touch them and no one ever looked me in the eye anymore—they couldn't get past the boobs. As I got older and started to date, it was a constant battle to keep guys away from my chest. I was so self-conscious about my size that I did anything I could to be unnoticeable.

Then one day I was watching TV when this adorable blond woman began singing an enchanting song. I listened intently to the words of her song, but couldn't take my eyes off her boobs … They were bigger than mine and she was a star! After she sang, she was interviewed and I was in awe of her openness, down-home warmth, and humor. She made no bones about her figure and she said, "If you got it—flaunt it. God gave us whatever body He chose for us and we gotta learn to love ourselves for who and what we are. I like myself, because God loves me!"

Tears started rolling down my cheeks as I realized that no matter what anyone else thought, I was a child of God's and He loved me.

He gave me this body as a gift and I should be proud of it—as He is of me. God knew the pain I suffered, but He was always with me and loved me through it all.

I will always love that great country singer and songwriter, Dolly Parton, as she was delivering a message that day straight from God to me … love yourself!

As Ecclesiastes 3:11a says, "He made everything beautiful in his time."

Elvis

I was never crazy over any performer as a teen. It seemed stupid to me how ga-ga girls acted over teen stars. In my mind, all that screaming and fainting was a dumb way to act. I was much more serious as a teen, but I liked music, especially Bobby Vinton, Bobby Vee, and Elvis.

Actually, it is strange how I became a devoted Elvis fan. It happened through my younger daughter, Lorie. Lorie was born just months before Elvis died, but when she was about five years old, we would sneak off to Chuck E. Cheese Pizza so she could put her tokens in the giant "Elvis" mouse. She would sing and dance along to "Hound Dog," "Blue Suede Shoes," and "Jailhouse Rock." She was adorable!

One day we went into our favorite Chuck E. Cheese and they had removed "the King"! From that day on, we never went back and we soon forgot about the King.

When Lorie was nineteen years old, she rediscovered Elvis and fell in love with him once again. She bought all of his recordings and we rented his movies to watch. Lorie loved *Viva Las Vegas* and *Blue Hawaii* the most. She could imitate his moves and facial expressions better than most male impersonators.

One day Lorie came to me and said, "Mom, I really want to go to Graceland with you and Julie" (her older sister). So I got this wild idea that it would be fun to create a new tradition—"the Girls' Vacation." This would be a once-a-year event when Lorie, Julie, and I would take off and have a short, fun girl's trip.

Our first trip was to Graceland, of course. Julie hardly recognized Elvis' songs, but Lorie changed that by playing Elvis's music during the entire trip.

It was a hot August day when we put the top down on my red Z28 convertible. Lorie sported a Miami Dolphins cap, Julie a San Francisco 49ers cap, and I wore my Cruella De Vil hat, which the girls said I needed because we drove in a similar fashion.

Julie and I quickly learned the words to Elvis songs, with a little coaching from Lorie.

We laughed, sang (off-key), and ate the entire time. We had so much fun that my ribs hurt for a week from laughing so hard. It didn't really matter what we were doing or what our destination—just being together was so much fun.

Julie's self-designated job was to point out *all* of the restaurants along the way and Lorie's job was to entertain us with her marvelous wit. Julie laughs so easily at everyone's wisecracks that she is a perfect traveling companion. My job was to drive and pay the bills. (Hey, I'm the Mom—it's my job!)

Very honestly, I don't believe that anyone can go on the Graceland tour and not come out with a new respect for just how much Elvis influenced the music world. I certainly gained a new respect and admiration for Elvis on that trip, and so did Julie. It was no longer just our love for Lorie that encouraged us to like whatever she liked, but we discovered our own genuine love for the King. The girls and I have always been close, and with this new common bond, the three of us formed yet another deeper bond and commitment for each other.

On the way home, I asked Lorie, "Honey, what drew you to Elvis—besides his good looks and great music?" Without hesitation, Lorie answered, "Mom, I am so impressed by his deep faith in God, his overwhelming contributions to charity, and his love and devotion to his mother." Now, how could I argue with that?

This trip became the first of many with my girls. We now have our "girls' vacations" twice a year and have fallen in love with Graceland as well as Las Vegas. Last year, my precious Aunt Norma joined us as she was always an Elvis fan. She officially became "one of the girls" on that trip as she laughs at all our silly jokes too!

Elvis brought music to this world like no other performer and carved the way for many to follow, but to me, Elvis brought me closer to my daughters and for that I say to him, "Thank you—thank you very much!"

Reba

Things were really tough for me when I found myself a newly divorced mother of three kids. I had to find a job as soon as possible, so I was answering every ad in the paper. I was especially interested in the one as a secretary at a local country radio station in Bakersfield, California.

That morning, I made sure my make-up was just right and every curl was perfect. With résumé in hand, shoulders back, and feigned confidence, I walked through the big heavy doors of that radio station. I walked over to the receptionist, who took one look at me and screamed!

Quickly, I looked around and no one else was there. She was in a panic, yelling "Oh my God! Oh my God!" She jumped up and ran through the double glass doors and disappeared.

"Okay," I thought. "I'm not sure what that was all about, but I think I'll just sneak out before she gets back." As I started to turn, four people came running out, yelling, "Reba! Reba! Reba!" I stopped dead in my tracks as they circled me. I thought, "I don't know what a 'Reba' is, but I didn't do it!"

The look of disappointment on their faces made me stand perfectly still. One minute, they were smiling, circling me, and now they were mad at me? What gives? I said, "Excuse me. I'm a little confused. I just came by to apply for the secretarial job."

They looked over at their cowering, red-faced receptionist and said in total disgust, "This *isn't* Reba McEntire, you idiot!" She burst into tears and ran back through the glass doors.

I asked, "Who *is* Reba McEntire?" One of them pointed to a picture on the wall, told me that the position had been filled, and then they, too, exited back through the glass doors.

I slowly walked over to the picture and there was the famous country singer, Reba McEntire, with a warm smile on her face and a sparkle in her eyes. Yes, I saw a similarity (many pounds ago) to me.

As time passed, I began listening to Reba's music and I loved her. I was so impressed with her music and genuine humor. Reba is not only incredibly talented, she is so pretty. I thought how great it was that someone thought I looked like her. Maybe, just maybe, not everyone thought I was "pretty ugly and pretty apt to stay that way!"

Reba is respected by her peers and admired by her fans. She has so much talent, yet she continues to be humble. She has a way of touching lives with her music, her acting, and her sincerity.

I realized while watching her on TV recently that the special sparkle I saw years ago in her eyes comes from her incredible sense of humor. Reba showed me that humor comes in many forms, but without humor and laughter in our lives, there can be no sparkle.

Reba became the epitome of what I want to be as a professional speaker. To me, being a good speaker means being authentic, sincere, and remembering that I am only the messenger to help audiences find solutions to problems. My role is to help motivate, educate, and inspire my audience to be all that God intends them to be.

Through all of the difficult and trying times in my life, I know that the two key ingredients that have seen me through have been my faith in God and my sense of humor. Reba's theme song is "I'm a Survivor." She sings, " ... *a single mom who works two jobs, who loves her kids and never stops; with gentle hands and the heart of a fighter, I am a survivor! Who I am is who I want to be."*

Well, Reba, I too have survived and will continue to do so with my faith and sense of humor intact. It is my hope for each of you reading this story that you, too, will learn to believe in yourself, accept the gifts that you have been granted, get closer to the important people in your life, and always keep a good sense of humor!

Sheryl Rudd Kuhn

Sheryl Rudd Kuhn, MRR, LMBT, CLL, owner of Inner Touch for eight years, works with individuals and groups that want to *nurture body, honor essence.* Sheryl has a Master's Degree in recreation and is a licensed massage bodywork therapist as well as a certified laughter leader. She has twenty-five years of experience as an educator. Using a variety of tools with a splash of fun creates the dynamic style she uses within her massage sessions and during speaking engagements and workshops. Her easygoing spirit allows for heightened awareness and spontaneous learning opportunities.

She has written poetry entitled "I Am a Woman" and "The Wild Woman I Am" that she presented at a Men Stopping Violence workshop and a university Women's History Month gathering.

Sheryl's passion is "helping people tune into their bodies." She believes the more we understand our bodies and the greater connection we have with our minds, bodies, and spirits, the better choices we make to help create healthier selves and a healthier world.

Sheryl can be contacted at: Sheryl Rudd Kuhn, MRR, LMBT, CLL
Inner Touch
735 Ben Cook Road
Sylva, NC 28779
(828) 586-1761
Fax: (828) 631-3671
innertouch@earthlink.net
www.innertouch.biz

Unhooking the Past

By Sheryl Rudd Kuhn, MRR, LMBT, CLL

My nails were stained red. Orange-red clay caked my fingertips. The sun's warmth surrounded me as a breeze gently whispered through my hair. I was resolutely digging a hole in the southern mountain soil. *I had to bury the past.*

The hole was big enough, wide enough, and deep enough, and today marked the eighteen-month anniversary of a very tumultuous relationship. It was time to end this once and for all. I needed to move forward. I was thirty-six, never married, and recently unengaged for the second time in my life. I had to do something different. Totally, one hundred percent different. I had to quit drawing the kind of man I did not need or want or desire.

This time, I had sought a therapist to help me re-discover myself, to put back the pieces I had given away and those that had been stolen from me. I felt stronger emotionally then I ever had, but very alone. This time I *would not* accept second best! I needed to work on me, to gain my self-esteem and strength. I needed to create a total me, who didn't *need* anyone in her life, but who *chose* someone. I'd spent a year trying to find me within this relationship, only to pick myself up when I finally realized the wedding was not going to happen. My therapist felt it was time for me to take action, to symbolize the ending of this relationship. I had ended it every other way possible, except through ceremony. Though I was familiar with the idea of ceremony, I'd never created my own. My therapist highly recommended at least one witness, and assured me I'd know what to do.

I chose my therapist as my witness. She had seen and experienced my darkness and my lightness and accepted me just where I was. We sat directly across from each other, her observing, me in total control. By instinct, there were specific items I deemed necessary to create the relationship's end. A picture of the two of us at Callaway Gardens was the main item. Beautifully back-dropped with a lush jungle of trees, we stood with arms wrapped around each other's waists, smiling brilliantly for the camera. Dreams of wedding dresses, a future forever, and maybe even children had filled my head that day. Today would be the end of those dreams. Forever.

I had brought the picture, scissors, a small stick with a thread and a hook on it, and matches. In preparation for the ceremony, I had taped the stick, representing a fishing pole, to his hand in the photo. The attached thread connected the pole and the hook, which pierced my heart. The symbolic representation was just as vivid and painful now as the reality had been. In the beginning he had hooked me. I had swallowed the tantalizing bait. It was now time for me to release the hook and sever that which had connected us. I took the hook out of my heart, thus unpiercing what had been pierced, and returned it to him—I meant him no harm and therefore allowed the hook to dangle on the end of his pole.

I took the sharpest scissors I owned and separated us by a clean cut—no shreds, threads, jagged edges, or strings. Clean and final. We were separated. I placed my image on the side of the hole I had so determinedly dug. I put his image in the hole, with the pole, at the bottom. I struck the match—then torched him! It didn't take long until the ashes appeared, his image cremated. I took the soil that was piled on the side and covered the remains, never to be felt, seen, heard, touched, or tasted again.

I was free. I was free of a relationship that did not support my royal spirit. The pain I had felt was gone through ceremony. I had experienced something I had created, something a witness observed, and something I was ready for. If I had done this months or even days before, the effect would not have been the same.

My therapist cautioned me that in leaving the past buried I had created an opening, a void. She told me it was necessary to fill the void up with what I wanted. "What do you want in a relationship?" she asked. My lips parted in a huge smile, and I began relating what I'd discovered years ago when answering this same question at a workshop. I still had the booklet I'd artistically crafted thirteen years earlier.

The characteristics of *"my dream man"* and my ultimate relationship flooded back. He would be loving, caring, honest, fun, and willing to both roll in the mud and go camping as well as dance in tuxedo and formal dress. I wanted to feel his love from across the room as our eyes connected. I wanted to be loved, unconditionally. I wanted to give love unconditionally. I wanted to be accepted as I am. I wanted someone to share the responsibilities of our lives together, supporting each other in whatever adventures we chose and whatever challenges came our way. Maybe we would even work together. I wanted to enjoy sunsets, sunrises, to feel free within that relationship. An interdependent relationship is what I chose. All those qualities packaged in a tall, handsome man who could physically carry me was the order I wanted filled, and one I was willing to wait for.

I closed my ceremony by expressing gratitude for the experiences this relationship had offered, for my therapist, for the beautiful day, for the guidance to create this ceremony, and for God, Goddess, all that is. I went home feeling more at peace than I had in the previous weeks, months, or last year and a half. I felt like there was something on the horizon for me, but patience was a virtue I'd have to develop.

I had begun teaching a continuing education massage therapy class at our local community college. I love teaching people about their bodies and had a group of individuals who were excited about learning. In the previous month, I had become certified to massage pregnant and laboring moms as well as infants, and tonight I would begin teaching some of those techniques. I opened the class, night two of an eight-week course, and asked if anyone had any questions or wanted to share their experiences in giving or receiving massage. As I answered questions, a new student walked into the room. A male, average height, nice build, and handsome. He apologized for his tardiness as he moved toward a chair. I welcomed him and his beautiful hazel eyes connected with mine.

Words continued to fall out of my mouth about massage while my brain attempted to identify what was going on with my body. It felt like opening an endless file drawer, desperately trying to find the correct file. Blood pumped quickly and loudly through my body. Tingling began at the base of my spine and connected with my brain. The brain took control and continued to pour out logical, understandable information in the form of words. *Does anyone notice what is going on inside of me?* I felt the blood rush to the skin surface. *Am I blushing?* The massage information was on automatic pilot.

My brain finally found the correct file: *my dream man!* The one I had asked for only twenty-four hours before. *Oh my God. I'm not ready. This is too quick,* I thought. *How was I going to deal with this man—my dream man?* "*Teach,*" I heard a faint voice calling me back: "*Teach.*" My brain and body reconnected. The world appeared the same; the students no different. I scanned their faces and did not see any signs of confusion, disbelief, or questionable looks wondering, "What is she thinking?"

After class, *my dream man* came up and shared with me that he was a registered nurse on the obstetrics floor at our local hospital and would be very interested in learning more about pregnancy, labor, and infant massage. "Aha," I thought. "We will have a connection professionally and get to know each other that way—this will be safe." We met several times over the next months, discovering we went to the same church and ran in the same circle of friends. Our paths had not crossed due to his twelve-hour night shifts and being a single parent to three boys. Our professional relationship turned into a partnership with two other people, and we opened a wellness center together. While working together professionally, a personal relation-ship developed. We learned we were both healing from past relation-ships. Although neither of us had given up on finding a new relationship, we had both chosen to do some healing alone and then pursue the relationship of our dreams.

Hikes, dinner parties, business meetings, church outings, and friendly get-togethers filled the year. Feelings I had wanted for so long and had not allowed began to surface. I had taken the time I needed to heal myself from past wounds and I was ready to seek a relationship with *my dream man.*

Valentine's Day eve, we decided to discuss our relationship, a discussion I initiated. I felt it was time to date or move on. I did not want to waste time in another relationship with someone who wasn't ready for a commitment. Unsuccessfully, I had looked for a Valentine's card that essentially said, "I like you; there could be more. I need to talk with you about this. I'm scared to death and know this is the right thing to do."

We spent hours sharing hurts, hopes, broken dreams, newly created dreams, and exactly what we were looking for in a partner. My list was being checked off one by one—this was perfect. I then popped the question. I was thirty-seven years old, never married, and not sure I wanted to have kids of my own, but neither was I ready to let go of that idea, so I asked, "Do you want more children?" His reply was, "I'd love to have babies with you." It took twenty-four hours and my therapist telling me "You realize he just asked you to marry him" before accepting that *my dream man* was finally here.

Two months later on a chilly evening, we drove on the Blue Ridge Parkway. He'd asked me to dinner and this was certainly not the way to the restaurant. As the car curved around the rocky walls of mountains, brilliant orange and pink filled the sky. He expertly turned the car into the parking area and asked me to get out of the car. Down on one knee he went, while my brain attempted to find the file again, blood pumping loudly and quickly, a tingle traveling up my spine. "Yes" sprang from my lips. We'll be celebrating our fifth anniversary this June.

I would never have been ready for *my dream man* or able to accept the unconditional love he offers if I had not unhooked the past. As I think about it, I realize I made five choices to unhook my past and allow me to get exactly what I wanted.

Committing to become a whole person prior to inviting a partner into my life was the number one priority. I knew if I continued to complete myself by needing to have someone in my life, I would continue to draw the same man and experience the same hurts. Through reading many self-help books, participating in female only and co-ed self-discovery groups, and being open to changes and possibilities, I became whole.

Second, counseling/therapy gave me the opportunity to explore my darkness and my lightness and accept all of me. A counselor/therapist whom you trust is important. My therapist guided while allowing me my process. She empowered me to close doors and open new ones, to feel the deepest darkest parts of me, to rejoice in the lightness, and to accept it all.

The ceremony I chose to do, with harm to none, brought the mental and spiritual into a physical plane. This third choice allowed me to access every sense I have and kinesthetically unhook from my past. This event was very powerful because I was ready. I had done a lot of work on my own and with my therapist. Without the groundwork and foundation, this ceremony would never have been successful. Timing is critical. I still have memories and thoughts about my previous relationship, but the ceremony released the emotional charge surrounding those memories. They are events in my past that helped to create who I am today.

The fourth choice was opening and accepting what I'd asked for. Every characteristic I asked for in a relationship came true, except two: his height and ability to carry me in his arms. I wasn't willing to sacrifice all the other qualities to wait for a man who was a few inches taller. Sometimes we have to re-evaluate our choices. The reason I wanted someone tall who could carry me, I realized, was to feel safe and secure. I had created that safety and security within me and had found other qualities within him that supported the same. He can't pick me up, but he carries me in many other ways, loving me unconditionally.

The fifth choice was trust, and this was a difficult one for me. First, control has to be let go of. I had dated many men in the thirteen years from when I'd initially written down the characteristics of my ultimate relationship to when I met my husband. I had tried to fit all the men I dated into those characteristics. None of them had measured up. There were periods of time when I felt very alone and wondered if I'd ever be married. I also had a grandmother who told me my expectations were too high. Through it all, I continued to hold on to my ultimate relationship and not accept any less. When I did accept second best, I was not myself. My royal spirit was squashed and hidden. I had written down my request and I had to trust. My trust was put in God, Goddess, All That Is, and I can't say that I was always patient. However, looking back over the events of my life, I needed to experience every one of them to be prepared for my ultimate relationship. Thirteen years seems like a long time, yet I know now it was all in divine order.

My own unhooking of the past took the form of a relationship. This same process can be used to unhook from a situation, car, friendship, deceased loved one—any event/object/person that holds an emotional charge for you. Accessing resources, being willing to do the work, accepting what you ask for, creating ceremony, and trusting combine to unhook the past. This is not an exclusive list. You may find more appropriate avenues for your situation and process. Whatever path you take, may you find that unhooking from the past renews and rejuvenates your royal spirit within!

ᴄ ᴄ ᴄ

Carolyn L. Larkin

Carolyn Larkin has the privilege of addressing international audiences worldwide, including AMA; International Business Forum, Germany; universities in Korea and Japan; "XX Taller Ingeniería De Sistemas," Santiago, Chile; ACEF and ASTD, Colombia; DiaDisc Congress and IFTDO, Brazil; and PDVSA II Foro Internacional, Venezuela.

Carolyn is president and founder of Human Perspectives International, Inc., an internationally recognized consulting, training, and product development organization, with offices in Minneapolis, Minnesota, and Laguna Beach, California, and representative offices throughout Latin America. She has taught at the University of California, National University, California state colleges, and the University of Minnesota.

As a consultant to international companies, Carolyn exudes energy and excitement and a deep sense of passion for her work. She is committed to sharing her life's work with cultures throughout the world. When not traveling or addressing audiences, you'll find her with her husband, family, and friends fishing in Minnesota or walking on the sand in Laguna Beach, California.

Carolyn is an avid reader and writer of poetry. Her first published book of poetry, *Headlines of My Life*, is in its second printing.

Carolyn can be contacted at: Carolyn Larkin
2669 Pala Way
Laguna Beach, CA 92651
toll free: (800) 861-3819
www.hpiintl.com

My Gifts

By Carolyn L. Larkin

*I*t has been said that "In the midst of the darkest storm, there exists the greatest light." Although I have not always been aware of this, I know deep in my heart that every challenge, every change, is a gift from God that we must find and unwrap. My journey to discover this began as a very young child. The storms I have weathered throughout my life have brought me many great gifts.

It was 1969, and my life was changing faster than the speed of light in spite of my holding on with "white knuckles." The storm began when my knight in shining armor "rode off on his horse" with another woman and I became an ex-wife. I was in shock, denial, resentment, and most of all resistance. I had four children under the age of eight, two were in diapers, and one was profoundly deaf and hyperactive. Eight insecure eyes looked at me every day, and the overwhelming responsibility scared me to death!

Facing the judge in divorce court with my four kids, one in each arm and one hanging on each leg, I was told, "You'll receive $100.00 per month child support, no spousal support, and $500.00 to help you move to a new residence." The shock of the verdict stunned me. I begged the judge to reconsider. Uncontrollable tears streamed down my face, but my pleas fell on deaf ears—not my child's deaf ears, but the judge's! I was also dealing with the reality that I would have to reinvent or, rather, reconstruct myself.

I felt my life was over! One hundred dollars a month child support was not much help. I knew I had to do something to deal with the reality, but what was I going to do? Who would help me? How was I going to make it on my own? How could I possibly take care of all these children? I felt I was just a kid myself, now alone with four kids, one with a multitude of health problems. I had no degree and had not worked for many years.

I kept asking God, "Why? Why, God?" I wondered what I had done to deserve this. The questions were endless, but there were no answers. I felt weak in the knees and physically sick to my stomach.

As a first step, I decided to return to California, my home state. I packed my dilapidated Datsun station wagon and began the drive from Texas to California. To say the least, we were quite a sight: four bewildered young children in the back seat of a beat-up car, with a zombie mother in a state of panic. I drank gallons of coffee along the way, while my fears kept sync with every heartbeat.

By the time I reached the border of Arizona, I was a total wreck. Fear had overtaken my body. I spent most of my time driving with tears streaming down my face, barely able to see out the car windshield. My eyes were puffy from tears and lack of sleep. With less than $500.00 to my name and four kids to feed and house, it was obvious to me that a restaurant meal or hotel room was an extravagance that couldn't even be entertained.

Telling the children the biggest "story" of my life, I convinced them that we were on vacation as we drove thousands of miles towards home. We camped out, cooked hot dogs, and enjoyed junk food. As we continued, we began to tell stories, sing happy songs, and create fantasies. I tried to make every stop an adventure, and every conversation with strangers along the way was filled with a sense of bravery and hope. This began to instill in me a feeling of achievement and my optimism began to grow with each new mile.

By the time we reached California, I was convinced that I could do anything. After all, I had just survived driving thousands of miles with four young children, cooped up in a car held together with cheap gas, cheap oil, bald tires, cranky kids, and a crazy mom with fear breathing heavily down her neck.

And then, navigating through a strong windstorm in the Laguna Mountains on the outskirts of San Diego, California, I was startled by a fierce banging on the roof of the car where the luggage was tied down. I stopped the car and turned off the engine. I didn't want the vibration of the luggage to awaken my deaf daughter, for then I knew she would be awake for the rest of the evening. Nothing could calm her down to sleep more than four hours a night.

I struggled against the forceful wind while I tried to see what the banging noise was. Too late, I realized that the wind had loosened our luggage from the car's support bars and was hurdling it down the mountainside.

Gift Number One

Instead of crying as usual, I began to laugh uncontrollably. I became hysterical as I saw our opened luggage tossed down the mountain with our clothes and underwear flying everywhere in the wind. Suddenly I could hear my Mother say, "Never leave the house without clean underwear. You never know when you might have an accident and have to be taken to the hospital."

Here I was, a divorced mother of four, with no home, no job, and a very gloomy future, laughing hysterically while all our clothes went flying down the mountain. My good Italian mom's advice was now the ironic joke of the year. My underwear was flying down the mountain along with all the rest of our clothes, and all I could do was laugh!

The laughter was calming, and I drove into San Diego with the sun rising and feeling a sense of renewal and release. It was empowering, and I decided we'd have a genuine restaurant breakfast while I made some tough decisions.

The children devoured pancakes and orange juice while I decided I would first drive up to the University of California at San Diego and apply for a job. Next, I would look for a house to rent close to work. I'd put a deposit toward a month's rent, with a promise to pay the balance when I received my first paycheck. Later we could afford to ship the furniture my ex-husband had left behind. The furniture wasn't much, but it was all we had. Finally I had a plan, a goal, and something genuine to look forward to!

Convincing the personnel department at the University of California that I could do "any job they had open" was quite another thing. "First of all," the personnel woman told me, "even if I wanted to hire you, I couldn't. We have a hiring freeze, and that means we are hiring no one at this time." However, I was desperate. Hiring freeze, or not, I needed a job. Furthermore, I wanted a job in the department of psychiatry.

The woman was adamant. I begged and pleaded. Finally, I took the woman out to my car. There, eight little eyes looked at her and she saw the evidence of why I so desperately needed a job. When she looked at those eight little eyes, the one child with a funny hearing aid on, strapped in a harness with a "wild look in her eyes," the woman sensed this was no ordinary request for employment. With a half smile, she promised she would do her best to find me "something." I told her that "something" was not quite what I needed. I needed a job specifically working in the department of psychiatry, as I was on the brink of a nervous breakdown and my kids were probably going to grow up psychotic, so I had to have a combination of job and therapy. Moreover, I had a child with special needs and her first special need was a sane mother.

Gift Number Two through One Million, and still counting!

I got the job, the therapy, and the education. My children have grown into wonderful adults and parents. I started a company headquartered in the United States that has expanded to Japan and Latin America. Today, the company is in sixteen countries. And, interestingly enough, my biggest gift came when I met and married the man of my dreams.

I have been blessed by receiving many, many gifts during my lifetime that I continue to unwrap and that continue to come. One such gift came to me several years ago. At the time, I was invited to speak at several universities in Japan and Korea. After I addressed students at Myongii University in Korea, my kind Korean hosts wanted to do something special for me. They suggested a day of shopping in It'aewon, an area in Seoul.

In It'aewon there are many street merchants who sell various goods, souvenirs, sunglasses, purses, and much more. These goods are displayed on trays and the merchants hover about waiting for customers to come. I approached one of the merchants and asked him if he spoke English. He nodded "Yes."

I asked him if he would direct me to a fabric store. He nodded "Yes" again and wrote "250" on a piece of paper. I graciously thanked him and went looking for the address, which I could not find on any of the buildings. I returned to the man and he was very pleased to see me return. I showed him the piece of paper and again questioned him about the address.

He looked at the paper and, with a big smile, crossed out the number and wrote "225." Again, I thanked him and turned to go looking for the fabric store. As I walked away, I suddenly realized that the number "225" was not an address. It was a price he was negotiating. I hurried back to the gentleman and asked him in sign language if he was deaf. He smiled broadly and with a look of total surprise signed, "Yes, I am deaf. We are all deaf here," and pointed to the other vendors.

"Are you deaf?" he asked. I signed, "No, but my daughter is deaf." He asked, "Didn't you like my price for the sunglasses?" Then I knew his "250" and "225" were his bargaining prices.

Another vendor asked, "Are there deaf people in America?" I was embarrassed to think they thought Americans were so perfect we could ward off even one of the most common, albeit vicious, of childhood diseases such as the rubella virus that had infected me and my child while in her embryonic state. To his innocent question, I humbly responded, "Yes, many, there are many deaf Americans." This was the beginning of a very heartwarming experience. For hours, the street vendors gathered around me and excitedly told me their life stories. Many graceful hands flew through the air and bridged the gap between two cultures. This provided me with yet another very precious gift.

My Special Gift

As a young child, my love for God gave me hope that God would lead the way to a happy life. As a divorced young mother, I often found myself wondering why God was punishing me. For years I cried and wallowed in my sorrow, wishing that I didn't have the burden of raising my children alone. I especially didn't want to deal with the challenges involved in raising a deaf child with a weak heart. There were many, many difficult decisions and surgeries, with long lonely waits in hospital rooms and intensive care units. Often I had to take time I should have spent with my other three children in order to fill this one child's special needs.

Finally, I realized God was not punishing me. God allowed special gifts to come into my life through my life experiences. My deaf daughter is one of those special gifts. Because of her, I was able to communicate with total strangers in a foreign country in a very special way. My ability to sign words opened the hearts of a group of human beings who wanted to communicate with me and I with them.

This gift was more than any trip, recognition, or applause. It was my special child, the child I often wished was not my burden, the child who taught me so much and made my family strong, the child who gave us the gift of communicating herself through sign language. Without that gift, my world would be smaller, I would be smaller, my life would be smaller.

Looking back on my life, I know deep in my heart that changes and challenges come to everyone, and every change and challenge in my life has been a gift to find and unwrap. I hope you will look at your challenges and find the gifts in them. Never, ever, give up. Underneath all that "stuff" and "junk" that life hands to you are very special gifts. Sift through the sands of your life, and find your unique and precious gifts.

A Gift for You

From Tracy with the Deaf Ears

Do you hear me when I'm talking?
Cause I've got a lot to say
And if you don't understand me
In my funny, garbled way

Could you possibly just listen?
And take notice in my eyes
When you see my teardrops glisten
Maybe then you'll realize

That I want so much to tell you
That you've done all that you can
If the words I say are mixed up
Then I'll tell you with my hands

You don't have to say you're sorry
You don't have to be ashamed
I am proud to be your special child
And proud to have your name

We have had our share of burdens
And the times were often rough
But the love and perseverance
Helped me be a little tough

And the courage that's inside
I feel gets stronger every day
If I stumble every now and then
It's a little price to pay

My Gifts *Carolyn L. Larkin*

You have taught me many lessons
And I'm sure I've been your guide
Cause together we have traveled
Walking closely side by side

So be proud that you've accomplished
All you have in every way
Yes, you took the time to listen
To the things I had to say

Mom, you took the time to listen
To the things I had to say

℮ ℮ ℮

Janet Luongo

*J*anet Luongo is flying high. Literally. SKY RADIO broadcast her vision of creative leadership on a special in-flight radio program, "Best Speakers in America," on 30,000 flights in 2002 reaching over 5 million passengers on American and Northwest Airlines. She is a co-author of *Mission Possible* Vol. 4 published by Insight Publishing, an anthology that includes Mark Victor Hansen, co-author of *Chicken Soup for the Soul*.

Luongo's paintings were exhibited in Paris and Geneva. She has written two novels and a play entitled *Our Father Who Art in Florida*, which she produced and acted in. As vice-president of education of The Discovery Museum in Connecticut, she produced five documentaries for Sound View public access TV, and her multi-cultural programs earned three state-wide awards.

An instructor of American Management Association courses, Luongo has taught art and communications in the U.S. and Europe at all levels, including college. She is a leader in the women's art movement, having founded a chapter of a national organization, Women's Caucus for Art.

Luongo is colorful and humorous as a presenter, specializing in creative leadership through her management training company, Open Minds Open Doors, LLC. She is president 2002–2003 of the New York chapter of the National Speakers Association.

Janet can be contacted at: Janet Luongo
Open Minds Open Doors, LLC
toll free: (877) 307-4486
janet@openminds-opendoors.com
www.openminds-opendoors.com

How I Got My Paintings to Paris Despite Stupid Bureaucrats

By Janet Luongo M.S.Ed.

When I was a little girl I loved drawing. I spent hours coloring pictures and looking at them. I dreamed of being an artist. My mother displayed reproductions by French artists, and we sang "Frere Jacques." When I was a teenager studying in art school, I found out that one of the centers of the art world was Paris. I loved to look at books that showed the paintings of artists like Mary Cassatt, Picasso, and Matisse. I looked at their studios, the boulevards they walked down, the cafes where they met, the galleries where they exhibited. I wanted so much to be there. I resolved that one day I was going to show my pictures in Paris.

I got closer to my dream when my husband Jim proposed that we apply for jobs abroad. I got a job in Japan; Jim got one in Switzerland. Japan or Switzerland? Jim debated but for me it was clear—everyone knows Geneva is a lot closer to Paris than Tokyo!

So did we go to Switzerland? Yes, and I invite you to come along.

There was a new train that could get from Geneva to Paris in three hours—the TGV. Jim and I visited galleries in Paris. I asked a few gallery owners if they would consider looking at my slides.

"No, Madame," they said. "We have all our expositions planned for the next three years." I fought off feeling discouraged.

I developed a plan. First I created a lot of new canvases. Then I was offered an exhibit at a local gallery in Nyon, my town on Lake Geneva. My strategy was to print the very best invitations I could afford and send them to better galleries, letting them know I was available for an exhibit in the future. All they could say was no, right? And that is what most of them said: "No."

All it takes is one gallery. One day I got a call from Madame Motte, who invited me to meet her at her *Gallerie*, one of the most prestigious in Geneva. Madame Motte was the *Grande Dame* of the art world, having started the first modern gallery in Geneva. On those very walls, she had hung works by Picasso. She had shown New York abstract expressionists. She said she knew Matisse, my idol. Then she asked to see my work. Nervously, I pulled out my slides. She looked slowly through my portfolio without saying a word. Then Madame Motte looked up. She said, "Would you like to have an exhibit in my gallery?" I thought, is this a trick question?

"Yes. Yes, of course I would like to exhibit my work at your gallery!"

It was truly wonderful. But Geneva is not Paris. Once again I sent beautiful invitations to my exhibit, hoping to show next time in the best galleries in Paris.

One day in the post a notice arrived that eight of my paintings had been accepted for an exposition in Paris! I was absolutely thrilled and spent a day celebrating with Jim and my friends. It was the start of an adventure!

The next day I have to figure out how I will get the works there. Jim helps me wrap them and we have to use two large boxes, each about five feet tall. We figure the least expensive way to transport them to Paris will be for me to take them up myself by train.

Jim packs our little Fiat with the boxes and drives me to the Geneva train station. Confronted with the dreaded customs forms, I cheerfully check off the box "Fine art." Destination? I write *"Gallerie, Paris."* For sale? *"Oui!"*

I declare that the works are "for sale," even though I will then be liable for taxes if they sell, because it makes me feel professional. I don't know my honesty will backfire. I proudly hand the *douanier* my papers.

The bureaucrat looks at my papers, looks at me, and says, *"Non, non, Madame."*

"What do you mean, *'Non? Non?'"*

"Non, you cannot take art for sale on the train."

"Why not? They are my works."

"Non, you must ship 'fine art' as 'fine art.'"

"Okay. How do I do that?"

"Il faut payer." He tells us the fee and Jim turns pale.

So much for being honest.

I beg him. *"Monsieur,* I must deliver them *today.* Don't you understand—this is an exhibit in *Paris."*

"*Impossible*," he answers.

I say, "Fine. I'll pay the fee. Give me the papers, *s'il vous plait*."

"*Non*, you must go to another office. At the other end of Geneva."

"Please give me directions," I say curtly, barely containing my rage. I am determined to get around him.

But now Jim says it is too late. He needs the car to go to work. He says there is no time to get the paperwork done and the work shipped before the deadline today.

"You got so close," he says. "There will be other opportunities," he reassures me. "We need to go home now."

I can't believe my ears. My head is pounding; my heart is broken. This petty bureaucrat is blocking me from having my exhibit in Paris, an opportunity of a lifetime.

Am I going to fight this? Yes, I am determined to find a way.

Thinking fast, I tell Jim, "Darling, give me the keys!"

He says, "What?"

I say, "You have to take the train back to work; there's one leaving in five minutes. I'm taking the car."

Shaking his head, he tosses the keys to me as he dashes off, yelling, "Call me! Let me know where in the world you wind up!"

"What now?" I ask myself. I find one of those luggage carts and push my packages towards the car park until I come to an escalator. I figure the Swiss are so efficient—watches, machines, cuckoo clocks—that they probably designed the escalator to accommodate the carts. Wrong. It gets stuck and the whole escalator grinds to a screeching halt. Commuters shake their fingers at me. These people are not helping me get my paintings to Paris. I slide the packages down the escalator and drag them to the Fiat and take off into the drizzly streets of Geneva.

Now where is this dumb bureau? I locate the area, but can't find the address. I ask someone.

"*Just-la*," the man says. "By the border."

I drive up to the guardhouse, but no one is there. It is a dreary raining day and the *douaniers* don't want to come out. I wait, wasting valuable time. Maybe I should go in and get them? Get them? It dawns on me that *I am at the border*. France is just ahead. No one is there to check my papers or my packages. Can I just drive through? I have never done that before. Is it legal? *France is just ten yards ahead of me.*

Tell me, do I drive through the border? Yes, I drive right through the border and into France.

Voila! Now I am in France. Now what? I have to be in Paris in just a few hours, before the gallery closes. Should I drive all the way there? I don't think I have time. Then I notice that the gas is low. I hadn't intended to be making a long car journey today. I remember that the TGV stops just once at the little French town of Beauregard before it takes off direct to Paris. I check the train schedule and, yes, it looks like I can catch the very same train that I would have caught in Geneva. I rip the map out of the glove compartment and locate Beauregard just over the mountain. I pull into the car park and then realize I need money to put in the meter and I have no French change. I run down to the station, but this is just a small town and there is no bank. I buy a roundtrip ticket but the ticket master has no change. There is a small restaurant that changes my Swiss francs for French francs. I run back up, put the money in the meter, and dash back down carrying one package and leave it there unguarded while I run back up and come back down with the second package. Whew. I drag both packages to the train track with just a few minutes to spare.

As I am waiting for the train I see a phone and think, "Oh, I better call Jim and tell him I'm on my way to Paris after all." I open up my handbag and reach in … and my wallet is not there! I check my pockets. No, my wallet is missing. I have no wallet! I probably dropped it running up and down. Just then the train pulls in to the station. It seems it's finally time for me to admit defeat and go home. The train stops and the doors open. I'm not that crazy to go to a foreign city with no wallet, no money, no I.D. Or am I? The train whistle blows. I get on the train!

In less than three hours I arrive with my paintings in Paris. I toss them off the train, but all the carts are claimed. Just then, I see Erik waiting for me. The son of a friend, Erik is a student in Paris whom I called to meet me at the station. I am so relieved to see him! He takes one of the packages, I take the other, and we heave them out to the rainy street and hail a taxi. My eyes and heart take in the beautiful boulevards, the *Arc de Triomphe*, just like in the art and storybooks. We get to the gallery in fifteen minutes. I admire the beautiful art in the room, take my receipt, and leave my paintings in good hands. I've made it—I've delivered my works to the gallery in Paris! This is actually the easiest part of the day.

Erik has enough money to buy some hot dogs and beer. I order two beers. I ask him for a twenty-franc bill, which I'll need to buy gas when I get back to the train station. I feel pleased, exhausted as I am, that I am thinking ahead. I want to call Jim, but the train is boarding. I cannot miss the return train. At Beauregard I claim my car and drive directly to the gas station. It is closed. That's okay; I anticipated that. That's why I asked for the twenty-franc bill. Gas stations in the Geneva area have machines that accept bills and allow you to pump gas yourself. Self-service. However, the gas station in Beauregard does not have this machine.

All I can do is drive in the direction of home and hope for the best. But because it is so dark, so stormy, so late, and I am so tired, I start going down the wrong side of the mountain. I find myself in an even smaller French village around midnight. No lights, no restaurants, and certainly no gas stations. I finally see a sign for the *gendarme* (that's like a sheriff in America). I ring the bell and soon a sleepy young officer answers.

"*Monsieur*, excuse me. I am lost. Telephone?"

"*Telephone? Oui. Entrez, Madame.*"

Remember, Jim has not heard from me since I left Geneva seventeen hours earlier. "Jim, I'm at the police station. Don't worry."

I hope the *gendarme* is going to be a prince charming and somehow conjure up some gas for me, give me a cup of coffee, and send me merrily on my way.

He says, "There's a gas station on top of the *montagne*."

I say, "*Monsieur. Vide.* Empty."

"*Pas vide,*" he says. "You have enough."

I am thinking, "How can you possibly know I have enough?" But what else can I do? It is raining even harder and trucks are whizzing past me. The red fuel light is furiously blinking and I think this car is going to die and a truck will push me into the ditch and who will know where I am? I have no ID. I am losing it now.

I pull myself together when I see the beautiful white gleaming light of the gas station. I fill up at the top of the mountain and roll back home to Jim.

Jim says, "You went through all that just for an exhibit in Paris?" Then he asks, "Was it worth it?"

What do you think?

A few weeks later …

Jim and I, with a full tank of gas, drive down the elegant boulevards to the gallery for my opening. We clink our champagne glasses, nibble the camembert, and listen to the music of Ravel and the murmur of French-speaking patrons discussing the color in my paintings. Dressed in jade green brocade, perfumed in Chanel # 5, I thank the American ambassador for coming to see my exhibit. It is a dream come true.

Afterword

I use my true story, "How I Got My Paintings to Paris Despite Stupid Bureaucrats," to teach many lessons: the importance of one's dreams, goal setting, risk taking, creative thinking, and the refusal to give up. All these qualities are attributes of a creative leader.

An excellent leader must have a strong vision of where she wants to go. She's got to see it, smell it, taste it, and hear it. If true passion is what drives her, she is unstoppable. She must have the confidence and courage to go on, even when she's afraid. She may have to go it alone for a while and bear the sneers of others. She may have to bend old rules that make no sense. She must not be deterred by roadblocks. Planning the trip is important, but if she gets sideswiped, a leader must be ready to take alternative routes.

If we want to transform culture and put our vision into action, women are realizing we must have the "guts" to lead. If we can't go through the mountain, we will find a way to go under it, around it, or over it. On our journey, we know how to engage the support of other people. And when we reach our destination, and all the stops along the way, we will make sure to take the time to celebrate!

ᴇᴏ ᴇᴏ ᴇᴏ

Joyce C. Mills

*J*oyce C. Mills, Ph.D., has inspired audiences with her playful and creative approaches to communication, problem solving, and healing. A consultant, workshop leader, and keynote speaker to health care, psychological, educational, community, and media organizations, Dr. Mills is an expert in the use of storytelling to communicate with severely troubled children and adults. In 1997 she received the Annual Play Therapy International Award for an "Outstanding career contribution to the field of child psychology and play therapy."

The founder and executive director of The StoryPlay™ Center, Dr. Mills is a certified and licensed marriage and family therapist with a Ph.D. in clinical psychology. She is also a registered play therapy supervisor and works with the Nana's Children's Mental Health Foundation, a non-profit organization in Phoenix, Arizona, which provides play therapy to homeless children. Dr. Mills is also on the board of directors of the Turtle Island Project, a non-profit organization in Phoenix, Arizona, and co-leads healing retreats for women with Native American spiritual and educational leaders. She currently provides workshops and consulting nationally and internationally and is in private practice in Scottsdale, Arizona.

Joyce may be contacted at: Joyce C. Mills, Ph.D.
The StoryPlay™ Center
El Dorado Square—Bldg. G-103
6609 N. Scottsdale Road
Scottsdale, Arizona 85250
Phone/Fax: (602) 923-2704
drjoyce@drjoycemills.com
www.drjoycemills.com

Whispers from God

By Joyce C. Mills, Ph.D.

"Utzie" is a Yiddish word describing a kind of itchy feeling experienced from the inside out. That's exactly what I was feeling while I was driving home from work along Kaua'i's lush north shore back in April 2001. It had been almost nine years since moving to Kaua'i, after twenty-six years of living in fast-paced Los Angeles. At that time, my husband Eddie and I had decided we'd outgrown a lifestyle that once seemed comfortable but now no longer nurtured us. We knew a move to such a remote island as Kaua'i was going to be a challenge, but at the time little did we realize the kind of challenge that was awaiting us.

On September 11, 1992, just ten days after our move, Kaua'i was devastated by Hurricane Iniki, the worst natural disaster to hit the Hawaiian Islands in the twentieth century. While in a shelter, I saw homes being lifted off their foundations, church steeples toppled, cars overturned, and huge banyan trees uprooted as if they were toothpicks. What began as a terrific adventure quickly turned into a living nightmare.

There was one particular moment when the winds were at their strongest—227-mile-per-hour gusts—and the concrete and cinder-block building in which we were harbored seemed to be swaying. Suddenly, with a deafening power and enormous force, the overhead steel and wooden louvers blew out, scattering debris everywhere. Moving quickly, everyone began to overturn huge cafeteria tables and benches to hide under for protection from the flying debris. Looking at the heaviness of those tables today, I don't know where my strength came from at the time. I could hear Eddie's voice through the roaring sound of the wind, calling for me to be careful and *get down*. For some unexplainable reason I was not concerned about getting hit by flying objects—things were happening too fast.

Eddie and I huddled together under one of the tables as the winds of Iniki continued with pounding force. It was during this breath-holding moment that tears came to the eyes of my husband, as he kept repeating in a somewhat mantra-like monotone fashion, "I know we've lost everything … I know we've lost everything." It was also in that tender moment of pain and fear over what seemed to be certain loss that a dream I had just before our move flashed through my mind like a bolt of unexpected lightening, electrifying my fear-darkened inner sky of thought. While remaining crouched under one of the overturned lunchroom tables and the thunderous noise of the wind continuing its pounding force, I decided to share this illuminating dream with Eddie.

I told him that about two months before moving to Kaua'i fear began to ripple through my body on a daily basis. My inner dialogue was going wild with thoughts such as, "Am I crazy to give up everything I know that has been safe and familiar? Am I nuts to move away from everyone I love, give up my home of twenty-six years, to move to a place we have only visited but never lived in? Where neither of us will have jobs or known sources of income?" These and other questions of fear began to surface more and more each day as the time for the move grew closer.

One night as I was restlessly lying in bed, I prayed for a dream that would help me through this time of fear. I felt like I was shaking the tree of faith for help … for faith in the decision to change the way we were living, to allow a possibility for new growth of self and soul. Finally, after a seemingly endless time of tossing and turning, I entered the place of the dreamtime and I was presented with the following gift:

I was walking toward a large field, perhaps one where a Native American ceremony such as a Pow-Wow has just taken place. Coming towards me were a man and a woman. The woman was carrying a large bird cradled in her arms. Only the tail feathers were showing, as the head was tucked under her arm. The man was carrying a large gray and white bird with a long neck and beautiful feathers. I recognized the woman's bird as an owl. I commented on how beautiful her bird was and said that the owl is a sacred bird in Hawai'i. I then went over to the man and said, "Oh, that's a medicine bird—it's very beautiful. You know, I go to these ceremonies and I would really like to have some feathers for a give-away to my relatives. So whenever you have extra feathers to spare, I would sure appreciate them."

The tall, kind man then moved closer and gently, with graceful, ballet-like hand movements, turned the bird over, reached underneath it, and held out two handfuls of feathers. Looking softly into my eyes he said, "Yes, this is a medicine *bird. Now hold out your hands." I did as the man asked, extending both of my hands. He then placed the feathers on the palms of my hands and said, "Here, they are called <u>Faith</u>, and you have all that you need."*

When I awoke, my hands were extended as I lay in bed and I found myself gently moving my fingers as if caressing the feathers placed there. I remained in bed for over an hour, thinking about what that dream meant to me. I realized that the man and the woman were messengers of both the feminine and masculine aspects of God. As I pondered their message, I believed it was telling me that while there were still many unknowns regarding the move for me to face, I was also being given the greatest medicine for confronting my fears: which was faith… faith in the form of the feathers. I remember feeling a deep sense of comfort and relief as I continued to reflect on the message of the dream.

After I finished telling Eddie about my dream, I noticed that he had extended his hands as if he, too, had received the feathers of faith in this moment of intense fear.

It was many hours until all was quiet once again. Together we ate, talked story, and slept on the floor, benches, and tables in the shelter until morning, when it was announced that it would be safe to go home.

Driving slowly through the hurricane-ravaged streets, we picked our way through downed power lines, destroyed homes, overturned cars, and toppled trees. As we rounded the corner to our street, which faced the ocean where waves had reached a reported thirty feet, my husband stopped the truck for a moment in fear of what we might see just ahead. Sharing in that same human moment the fear of what might have been lost, the message of my dream streamed through my consciousness as powerfully as the sun shines its rays through the windows of the clouds. I then reminded Eddie of the dream and its message that we have all that we need to confront our fears lying within the palms of our hands ... *faith*. Once again the message of faith outshined the grip of fear.

As we approached, we saw that our roof had blown off, there were many trees downed, and there were dead fish and debris strewn everywhere, but our home? It was miraculously standing! Our little tin-roofed, single-walled, glass louver-windowed home, standing just a few hundred feet from the powerful ocean, had survived the most ferocious storm to hit the Hawaiian Islands. How or why? I cannot answer such questions. I only know that it did.

What have I learned over the years from this experience? While I am still pondering that question for myself, I can tell you what I have learned thus far, and it is this: All of us live through hurricanes in one form or another, and there are many kinds of shelter in which we can seek safety from these personal storms. However, the most powerful shelter of all is built within the human soul. It is called *faith*.

Over the next nine years, our many personal storms continued. It became a daily struggle to get back on our feet professionally, financially, physically, and spiritually. Friends who had known us for more than twenty years repeatedly encouraged us to move back to the mainland, saying it was time to know when to give up the struggle. At this point, my husband was ready; I was not ready, yet I didn't know why. I kept saying that I'd know when I know: I'd see the signs. Something would speak to me. Friends laughed, saying, "Isn't losing everything enough signs?" For whatever reason, I wasn't ready to hear what they were saying, or see the signs the way they did.

Native elders tell us, "You hear the messages when you are ready to listen. You see when you are ready to look." Perhaps, on this particularly balmy April evening, while driving home along Kaua'i's luxuriant north shore, I was ready to both listen and look. During these quiet moments, I began to ponder, "Why can't I be satisfied? I live on one of the most beautiful islands anyone could imagine. I have a job that pays the bills and contributes to society. So what if it isn't exactly what I want to do. I have been married to a very loving husband for over thirty-seven years. We have two grown sons, a daughter-in-law, and grandchildren. I have had valued life lessons while living here, along with making special friends. One would think I have it all ... love, friends, home, job, and career. So what am I looking for? Why can't I be satisfied? Why can't I be grateful? What's all this *utziness* about?"

As I contemplated these questions, an old Talmudic teaching tumbled into my mind. It says, "God bends down and whispers to a blade of grass, *"Grow! Grow!"* I remained silent and continued to listen: I literally heard the whispering.

Like a lotus flower slowly unfolding its petals into full blossom, I gradually realized that my feelings were not about satisfaction, but instead they were about personal growth. I also realized I was confusing satisfaction and gratitude. Gratitude is about thankfulness; satisfaction is about fulfillment. I am always grateful for all of life's gifts, but I realized that I had not felt fulfilled in quite some time. In truth, I had gained over forty pounds while living on Kaua'i and my income had decreased significantly year by year, though I was working harder than ever. I was disconnected from my spiritual supports and the ceremonies that sustained and supported my soul's growth. Whatever professional seeds I had tried to plant hadn't grown. I literally felt a spiritual drought, while living in the middle of what is considered to be a paradise of moisture and beauty.

In those reflective few moments of solitude, I recognized that my feelings of dissatisfaction—*utziness*—were a powerful reminder for me to evaluate where I was in my life and to decide if I wanted to stay where I was or move forward towards a new direction. I knew it was clearly time to move forward.

Finally, after almost nine years of stressful living, I realized it was time to let go of what was once our dream and move back to the mainland. With tears in my eyes, we put our little tin-roofed, single-walled, glass louver-windowed home up for sale.

After considering many different places to move, we decided on Phoenix, Arizona. I had been traveling back and forth to Phoenix for close to two decades for both business and pleasure. I had co-led women's healing retreats yearly with Native American women for women from all walks of life since 1987. Both my husband and I had friends, relatives, and possibilities for new opportunities there. It was a place that had always nurtured my soul.

On August 13, 2001, we arrived at the home of dear friends who had graciously offered us a place to stay until we found a home of our own. Aside from our concern about being able to find a home we could afford, I only had one prerequisite for a house: I had to see "pretty." After all, even though our home on Kaua'i was very simple and small, we had lived across the street from the ocean, surrounded by astounding beauty. Of course, I knew that the desert would be different. But I also knew it holds its own beauty. Therefore, being close to nature and seeing beauty was important to me.

As it is when we open ourselves to the spiritual path, within three days we found the perfect home within clear view of a beautiful mountain preserve. We closed escrow without a hitch within fourteen days with the help of what I call a "real estate angel." We can see the sun rise from our back windows and watch it set from our front door.

As I contemplate this latest chapter in my life, I know there are many lessons yet to be learned from all of the challenges and personal storms placed before me. What they are, I do not yet know. However, now with *feathers of faith* in hand, whenever I experience that *utzie* feeling once again, I take a breath, close my eyes, smile, and listen to the whispers from God encouraging me to *Grow! Grow!*

This chapter contains original material and partially excerpted material from the book *Reconnecting to the Magic of Life* with permission from the author and publisher, Joyce C. Mills, Ph.D. Imaginal Press: Phoenix, AZ.

⊘ ⊘ ⊘

Rebecca Pace

ebecca Pace is a stimulating leader, dynamic seminar instructor, and a hilarious keynote speaker. Rebecca holds an audience's attention with her funny and entertaining analogies that create tangible learning experiences in her presentations. She delivers seminars and keynote addresses that are packed with energy, humor, and core skills that translate into corporate America.

Rebecca has served as an instructor at Tidewater Technical College and provided training programs and workshops for industry leaders such as General Electric, Telos, and Circuit City. Companies have requested Rebecca's unique presentation style on subject matters ranging from leadership, diversity, and Life Orientation all the way to building better workplace relationships. She is an active member of the National Speakers Association and the American Society of Training and Development in addition to the American Management Association.

Rebecca moves many with her message of "Falling forward while building your wings on the way down" in her sought-after keynote addresses. Her belief in self-esteem is clearly a required ingredient and is demonstrated in her presentation style. Rebecca teaches methods that encourage others to embark on a journey to rock solid self-esteem.

Rebecca can be contacted at: Rebecca Pace
4460 Oceanview Ave., #A
Virginia Beach, VA 23455
(757) 363-0191
RPace64@aol.com
www.r-pace.com

Snakes, Camels, and Courage, Oh My!

By Rebecca Pace

I was surprised by the luxury of first class on international flights. I was excited to have one of the big blue leather seats that recline and receive all the fuss and attention from the stewards on my flight to India. As I settled into my space, I begin to think that it was a real feather in my cap, not to mention a career booster, to have been selected from the available candidates to teach this overseas assignment. I was even impressed with myself for pulling off such a coup. The head of the training and development division of the company, my personal nemesis Debra, had approved me for the job. As I left American soil, I was truly thrilled with just how my life and career were shaping up and what my future would hold. I could just envision my nemesis granting the promotion that I had been coveting for the past eight years when I returned to the U.S. with international training experience.

As I looked about the plane, I noticed that I was seated around people who seemed to be much more seasoned at world travel than I was, so I observed their actions and followed suit. I drifted in and out of sleep, watched the movies on my personal mini-viewing screen, shopped the duty free merchandise, strolled through the plane on a journey into coach class, and returned to my deluxe seat to daydream about what treasures lay ahead in India. I also spent some time going over a mental inventory of everything I had packed that would temporarily make India my home away from home. Other expatriates had warned of what valuables would sustain me in a third world experience.

I awoke from dreaming about calculations on the amount of hand sanitizer I had packed just as we were touching down in France. I only had two hours to change planes and grab a souvenir. Upon entering the main terminal in Paris, it was obvious to me that Americans are mostly American. The airport was packed with many different nationalities and my mind was slammed with all the different languages and customs of different cultures. The Paris airport was a wake-up call that I was definitely not in Kansas anymore, and I really hoped my ruby slippers would arrive safely tucked in my luggage so I could slip them on for a little heal clicking if the need arose. I was beginning to see myself through very different eyes. I wondered if I had the courage and the strength of spirit to overcome the cultural barriers that I was sure to encounter. Had research equipped me for the task at hand, or would I need to call on Glenda, the good witch, to transport me back to my comfortable American world? What would clicking my heals three times do to help me deal with emotions when all that I knew and relied on was null and void?

This subject would require more exploration in my down time, but just the thought of it was pretty scary. I successfully boarded the second leg of my journey bound for India. I don't know what I was thinking, but I had expected the stewards and pilots to be American. They were not, and we all had to adjust quickly to the accents. It was interesting to see the menu in ten different languages, and comical for the Austrian steward to interpret my southern Texas-accented English as I made my meal selection. I was beginning to see the value in becoming multi-lingual. I was experiencing cultural hurdles, and I was not even off the plane! What a world, what a world! I had been told that the people I would be training with would speak English, but what language would my new hairdresser speak or how I would order food or give instructions at the dry cleaners? I slept a good portion of the flight in an effort to make up for the time zone change of ten and a half hours.

Dawn was barely cresting the clouds as the plane began its decent into India. I was here. The traveling was over; the journey was beginning. I was joyous over the circumstances and the benefits that teaching in another culture would bring my career, though I was clueless about the bounty India was to give me as an individual. It took twenty-four hours to get there, and the things I was about to learn about myself would last the rest of my life.

I peered out the window of the plane while waiting to deboard; the view did not seem that different or exciting from the tarmac, but that all changed when I left the familiar and headed inside the terminal in New Delhi. The smells of foreign soil hit me first and my senses were overloaded with all the aromas of spices, people, livestock, and a different way of life. It was confusing to hear a tongue so different from my own and to read display boards with English as the third language, but I proceeded with the flow of the travelers. My eyes explored the dark, beautifully mysterious people of India dressed in beautiful bright colors of silk and cotton. Everyone was so petite and exotic looking.

The Indian people were as shocked by my full-figured frame wrapped in leggings and an oversized sweatshirt as I was by their petite frames wrapped in brilliant colors. I exited customs with the world around me gawking and rushed to my destiny only to discover my first hiccup in the journey.

I had made it to India, but my wardrobe had not! Dazed and overwhelmed for a moment at the thought of no clothing or toiletries, I wondered what I would do. I felt certain there was not a Dillard's just down the street at the local shopping mall. I recovered from the momentary setback by rescuing myself with the thought of a trip to Emerald City in India. A shopping spree would be a treat and I do love to shop, anytime and anyplace. I placed a claim for lost luggage and looked around for an exit route. As I merged with the flow of foot traffic, I was taken aback by the military presence in the airport. Soldiers in the airport were a very fresh and alarming concept to me in 1999. I noticed the other travelers were not alarmed by their presence, so I discontinued my gawking and continued with the flow of foot traffic bound for an exit leading to the exotic world of India. I emerged into a large open fenced area that resembled a ball field diamond. I was amazed at the sheer number of people crammed into one place and was consumed with the loud, enthusiastic welcome in a foreign tongue. It was dawn, there was a misty, red haze in the air that I could not readily identify, and it seemed that everyone in India was at the airport.

I began to search for Carlson. He had arrived in India three days prior to me and had insisted on retrieving me from the airport. We had bantered about his chivalry, but I was thrilled he had won out when I heard him calling my name over the roar of a foreign tongue. Carlson was my knight in shining armor when he pulled me out of the crowd and spoke some of my beloved English. Coming face to face with a third world culture so totally different than my own via a fifteen-minute airport transition was overwhelming to say the least. I was surprised at my inability to just roll with the change; clearly I was not prepared for my destiny.

On the drive to what was to be my new home for the next eight weeks, Carlson familiarized me with details of our residence and what to expect. While he was talking, I took in the view out the car window at India. I was really here, and I was in shock at the visions meeting my eyes. Actually, I laughed a little at myself, at my naiveté that a three-thousand-year-old culture was perceived by me to be new. We continued the journey towards my new home and I discovered that I must adjust my vision and begin to live as something more than just an American. However, I was really glad that I had been conceived on American soil and by birth right grew up with central air-conditioning; the heat was killing me.

Just outside the car, my view was challenged by a gorge of dump trucks hauling a variety of items. The trucks were covered with Hindi script that I did not comprehend and some had old shoes hanging from the rear axle. I was told that the shoe was a Hindu custom for warding off bad spirits. What bad spirits? I just wanted to know what it took to ward off the 123-degree heat. As we drew near the inner city, it was stunning to see hundreds of homeless people camped out on every available patch of land, cooking over cow dung fires, bathing themselves, feeding their babies, milking buffalo, chasing away the pigs, getting hair cuts, and getting ready for their day. The sights made me wonder if I was anywhere close to having the strength and courage I needed to meet the opportunities that India provided.

At last we were at the guesthouse. Carlson advised me to go straight to sleep and avoid jet lag. Sleep seemed an insane suggestion. I wanted to explore my new neighborhood, not sleep. Digging through my travel tote, I wondered if I had packed all that was needed and how I might make ends meet until my luggage was located. I truly felt the need for a magic wand, a tiara, or something to give my sagging royal spirit a boost. I dug some jean shorts out and hit the streets for a self-guided tour of my surroundings.

Exiting my living quarters in shorts sent the entire male staff of the guest house into shock. I don't think they had ever seen a woman travel about loose on the streets of India in jean shorts or without an escort or at least a family member. So, off I went, heading down the street in my neighborhood, leaving them to gawk. At first I thought, this is not so different; I can do this. Hindu people were out watering their yards and getting their children off to school. The neighborhood was fairly new and the families who lived there were India's upper crust. The architecture looked a little different than I was used to, as did the cars, but it was nothing too shocking. I passed my neighbors and said "Hello," and I assumed they were saying hello back in Hindi. I don't speak Hindi, and I later learned they were saying, "Look at that big American woman in short pants; what is she doing in the street dressed like that!"

Clueless, I continued on my journey, hoping my luggage would show up soon. I noted two large sticks lying across the road. I wondered about those sticks because I had not seen trees anywhere near, but I kept moving on my foot journey. I noticed beautiful flowers and I saw some that were similar to the ones I grew up with in Texas. Cannes and portulaca were blooming in vibrant colors everywhere, and they were a little something from home to pull courage from. I drew closer to the sticks and was surprised to find them moving a little bit. I wiped sweat from my brow and decided they were a mirage. I had been tricked by many a mirage in Texas. Children playing in a puddle stopped to stare at me as did the woman carrying a basket of laundry on her head. When I looked at them, the children and the woman quickly averted their gazes.

This was to be my first dance with the caste system in India, which I found to be not much different emotionally than racism in America. I was distracted from these sad thoughts when I met up with my mirage of sticks and realized it was really two large, long cobras sunning themselves. I panicked! I am terrified of snakes. They raised their royal heads into the strike position and in cobra told me to get lost. I froze; I don't speak cobra! My Indian neighbors saw my terror and tried to rescue me, but I don't speak Hindi either. So, I went with what my English speaking senses were telling me. I heard the language of fear instruct me to *run!* I do speak the language of fear on occasion. I took off running as fast as I could. The snakes followed as fast as they could. My lungs felt like they would explode in the 123-degree dry heat of India.

As I ran with wobbly knees of fear, I recanted all the comments I had heard from friends and family about making this journey to a third world country to enhance my career. I recalled the doubtful comments about safety issues and the sheer madness of third world travel and living. Why had I not just settled down, married, and had kids? If I had, I would not be out here running from killer king cobras that were loose on the streets of India.

I looked over my shoulder to see if I was putting any kind of gap between me and the snakes. Nothing in my research had prepared me for camels. Who would have known that sometimes the camels in India roam freely about? While looking over my shoulder at the distance between the snakes and me, I failed to see the camel step in my path. I plowed full tilt right into the southern end of it, an experience that took aromatherapy to a whole new place.

On impact, I was laid out on the hot gravel street, legs cooking on the boiling rocks, with camel funk all over my person. It was disgusting. I was hot, tired, scared, and looking for snakes when I recovered from the impact. I never imagined that I would be grateful for camel funk, but I was. The funky scent derailed the snakes from their attack position and bought me safety. I didn't remember snakes or camels loose on the streets of Kansas … There truly is no place like home! Where, oh where, were my ruby slippers? Instead of heal clicking, my new friends ignored my camel cologne, my fear of snakes, and jean shorts on my full figure; they simply helped me off that boiling gravel and showed me friendship.

Finding my bearings, I made it back to the guesthouse and placed a call to my father to share the unbelievable first forty-five minutes in India. As the conversation was winding down, he asked me what I had packed to keep me safe and if there was anything he could send to aid me in maintaining my safety … something like snake repellent? I told my father that I had brought to India the same thing I always take with me everywhere I go. My Dad began to lecture me on the virtues not found in some good luck charm.

I responded in a royal voice, "Dad, I brought *me* and that has always provided the amount of courage and strength I need to survive life." We said goodbye with my father chuckling at the wonders of his daughter. I smiled at discovering that strength and courage were elements that all my sisters have and use to sustain the royal passage called life.

❧ ❧ ❧

Lori Palm

*L*ori Palm is a modern-day Muse inspiring passion and possibilities. She guides clients on a discovery journey, exploring the vision that reveals their hidden core passion. Lori uses a transformational three-step process that is woven throughout all her programs: *Exploring the Vision:* Finding Your Authenticity; *Weaving the Energy:* Creating Your Future; and *Creating Alchemy:* Living Your Destiny.

With her highly successful program, **Path To Passion**, Lori speaks at gatherings and works with groups and individuals using a magical process connecting people with their passion and allowing them to discover who they truly are.

Lori facilitates outward journeys to find the inner self through inspirational adventure travels to sacred sites around the world. Explore mystical ruins, hike in the rainforest, experience a sweat lodge ... **Heart Opening Journeys** helps people to discover new visions, explore possibilities, and create new patterns for their lives and businesses.

Using her highly developed intuitive skills, Lori weaves the seen with the unseen to guide people and businesses in developing a plan for themselves and their future.

Lori can be contacted at: Lori Palm
Palm Productions, LLC
Personal & Professional
Development for the 21st Century
(763) 595-8223
www.palmproductions.com

Crossroads on the Path To Passion

By Lori Palm

When a path closes and one stage of our lives is complete, we come to an *intersection*, a *threshold*, a **crossroads**. As we approach the crossroads, the inner stirrings begin. Something doesn't feel quite right. You can't put your finger on it, but you have a sense of impending change. During this time of uneasiness, you might have feelings of boredom, flights of fantasy (running away from it all), anxiety, depression, or even physical disease. And then all of a sudden one day, you don't even know who you are. You used to know, but now you're not so sure. It was over six years ago when I came to that crossroads and realized I didn't know who I was anymore.

And so the journey began … the journey to find *me*.

When a path closes, it feels like we're dying because our identities are threatened. When it happened to me, the stories about how I saw myself didn't fit anymore, but I didn't have any new ones with which to replace them. I thought of myself as a mom, a wife, a daughter, a business owner. Those words described my relationship with others, but who was I, not defined by anyone else? I had become what I thought everyone wanted me to be and, in the process, I had lost me. I realized I had submerged many parts of myself and that I had no idea where they were. I felt paralyzed, like a deer in the headlights—I knew something was coming, but I couldn't get out of the way.

On the surface, everything in my life looked fine. I was married to a good man, my two sons were out of high school, and I owned my own business. Everyone around me thought I was crazy for feeling so lost. But I was *not* having a breakdown; I was experiencing a profound shift in how I viewed the world. As I approached that crossroads, I did not regret anything that had happened in my life up to that point. It was all as it needed to be, but I also knew that my life going forward would look very different. I had no idea how it would look, but I felt driven to find out why I was here and what I was supposed to do.

When we're at the crossroads, what *was* falls apart … and what *will be* has not yet emerged. We're about to step into the *void*. I remember it so clearly. I felt like I was stepping off the edge of a mountain into thin air. I had no idea where I would land or even if I would land. I went into solitude, exploring "what was" … "what is" … "what could be." I believe we always have choices and so I had to choose. Did I want to stay in the rut, believing that I must be who I always had been? It was my choice—to stay in the pain of procrastination or to move into the possibilities of passion. I knew what I had to do, but I couldn't imagine how I would ever do it. I also knew that if I stayed where I was, I would get sick, probably cancer, and die. Finally I got the courage, and I stepped off the edge of the mountain, believing the wind would support me.

I jumped into the void with faith and one month's rent. At forty-seven years old, I left a marriage of twenty-five years to live by myself in a one-bedroom apartment. I believed I just needed some time by myself to sort things through. I needed to redefine myself. I had never lived in an apartment or even lived by myself before. Feeling guilty for leaving, I took very few of my possessions—a dresser, a desk, a few dishes. I even had to borrow a bed. I owned my own business and it wasn't doing very well because of all the stresses in my life, so I moved my business out of the office I was sharing and into the dining room of my apartment. It was a large first floor apartment with a sliding glass door out to a tiny patio, and it became my place of sanctuary. I didn't have a table or chairs at first, so I set my desk up in the dining room to look out across the living room and out the big window and sliding glass door. This '70s apartment (complete with harvest gold appliances) was surrounded by mature trees and a little pond. Sitting at my desk, all I saw were huge pine trees. I felt like I was safe, nestled in a cabin in northern Minnesota. My financial resources were meager, but I will never forget the feeling of total trust, knowing I was doing what I needed to do and knowing I would be okay, knowing I could take of myself.

As I stepped into the *unknown*, a deeper knowing of who I am came first. During those first months, I didn't have a couch or a comfortable chair to curl up in. I'm a pianist, and for the first time in my life, I didn't even have my grand piano. I would sit on the floor and meditate and just *be*. For most of my life, I had always been busy *doing*, and I realized that if I were going to find those lost parts of myself, I would have to be quiet and listen to the whispering of my soul and just *be*. Many times, just before we come to the crossroads, we fill our lives with busyness so we don't have to listen to that little voice whispering in our ear. When I stopped and began listening, my inner voice started to answer those questions I had never been able to voice before.

Two weeks later I took another leap. I went to visit my friend Pamela in Sedona, Arizona. I had no money for an airline ticket, but I had airline miles that were about to expire. This coincidence was the start of using the magic of conscious intention.

A window of consciousness was about to open. When I arrived at Pamela's home, there was a large painting sitting in the bedroom I was to stay in. I was immediately drawn to the wisdom I saw in the face of the native woman in the painting. Pamela explained that the artist was connected to the angelic realms. This original oil painting depicted an old native woman spinning threads with shining dots of light embedded in and around the threads. I had an inner knowing that each dot of light was a person or experience. Pamela explained that the old woman was the "webweaver" of the tribe because she weaved and connected people and experiences together. She was an important and honored master in the tribe. Pamela insisted that I take the painting.

"Why?" I asked. She smiled and said, "Because you are the "Webweaver," weaving people and experiences together." Gosh, could this really be a clue to who I was?

I began to understand that Pamela was showing me a symbol of who I was. At first when I looked at the picture, I believed it represented me, but I couldn't identify with it. As I pondered and allowed this new symbol of my identity to integrate into my life, I started to create a new story about me, about my gifts, and about my destiny. I began to own my gifts and to understand them in a new way. I started to become the Webweaver. I hung that symbol of me on the wall right behind my desk, and the energy of this image was so powerful that everyone who saw it asked if I would tell the story of the painting. The more I told the story, the more I became the Webweaver.

I believe I was given that symbol because I was willing to discover who I am. I realized then that I had been connecting people together and weaving energy my whole life—that it was not new. The new perception was seeing myself as a unique, powerful being with important work to do. I felt I was on my spiritual path connecting to my royal spirit, but I didn't know where I was going. I did know that as long as I stayed on the path, I'd be okay. All new and original thought begins with a focused question, which leads to an exploration. Our answers are all around us, but if we don't ask the questions, we will never begin to see and hear the answers. Questions can be dangerous— they require tremendous courage to ask because new questions lead to new ways to perceiving. My Adventure was beginning . . .

As I chose to become the "Webweaver," my life and my business started to shift. In the previous five years, I'd owned a speaker's bureau and had co-produced two cutting-edge conferences relating to breast cancer and menopause. I was also consulting with people about positioning and marketing their businesses. During those first few months, I meditated on not only who I was, but as the Webweaver, I wanted to know what I was supposed to do. One of the things I kept seeing was visions of traveling and working with people all over the world. Within those first six months, I went on a Caribbean cruise assisting one of the speakers I represented. Because I was inspired after my first trip to Sedona, I created *Heart Opening Journeys* as the inspirational travel division of Palm Productions and four months later took a group of fifteen people to Sedona for a transformational journey with an intuitive teacher. All this happened during a time when I had very little money, but it didn't matter because divine guidance provided everything I needed. Since my first trip to Sedona, I have taken many people to sacred sites around the planet, guiding them on an outward journey to find the inner self.

I believe I was creating my reality. I began to realize that most of the time we do it unconsciously, but I started to see that I could create what I wanted, what I felt called to do. I began to understand the cycles of life. I began to understand that we move from tradition to transition to transformation and that, ultimately, transformation becomes tradition and the cycle continues. You can't get from tradition to transformation without spending time in transition (being in the void).

Two months after I moved into my apartment, I received a contract to partner and set up a speaker's bureau with a local technical college. I was so excited! I believed I would have more resources and collaboration to do what I was already doing. I agreed to put all my speaking business through the college to build a bigger business. Within a couple of months, I realized I was back in the same old place of having other people leading my life and I was becoming who they wanted me to be. I had gone from transition back into tradition in terms of my work. It was a familiar energy and, of course, I knew how to work within the system. That's where I had lived most of my life. For the next twelve months, I kept trying to make this new position work because I felt I could always make everything work. Painfully, another leap was occurring and I had the courage to say, "This is not how I choose to live my life."

We ended this partnership on very good terms (never burn your bridges) and took my speaker's bureau back under the fold of my own business. I went back into transition regarding that part of my work to understand how I could move into transformation.

I continued to explore this huge question, "Who am I and what am I here to do?" New answers would appear as I was ready to hear them. About two years ago, I rented the movie *The Muse*, which is a comedy about Hollywood writers losing their artistic edge and finding their passion through the inspiration of a muse. As we watched the movie, my friend said, "Lori, that's you; that's what you do. You inspire people!" Many of the muse's traits were exaggerated in the movie, but I identified with most of them, right down to the muse's need to have the right conditions in order to have a restful sleep. Now I had another image to help me understand who I am. I started exploring and researching the Nine Muses and learned that in Greek mythology, the Muses were believed to inspire all creativity and to be the wellspring for all inspiration. They call us to find our authenticity, to explore our gifts and talents, and to meet our destinies. Clearly, the Muse was another symbol for me.

I realized I had come to another crossroads on my path and chose to once more go into the void. It was again a time of inner reflection and being still. After much soul searching, I chose to accept and integrate the muse, to actually call myself a modern-day Muse. As the Muse, I love helping people find their passion and exploring with them how they can make money doing that. I discovered that by integrating the muse within me, I help others connect to their own inner muse. My passion is to inspire my clients, but still I found that something was missing for me.

With excitement and apprehension, I re-entered the void, trying to find the missing piece. At that place of inner knowing, I reflected on the possibilities. I spent several days in the void before I could accept the next missing piece, which was to surrender old beliefs about myself and say, "I will never again say I don't do _____ (fill in the blank)." In the past, clients would ask me if I was a speaker.

I always answered, "No, I only represent speakers." Frequently I was asked if I was a writer, and again I always answered no. I also said I would never get married again. I embraced my passion and finally said, "I will do whatever I am called to do with whoever comes into my path."

I am now a speaker and an author. Following my passion, I work with groups as well as individuals in my program, **Path To Passion,** using a magical process connecting people with their passion and allowing them to discover who they truly are. As I move forward on my path, I continually encounter new crossroads and consciously enter into the void to find deeper levels of who I am and what I am here to do. And, by the way, I just got married to my life partner in a magical, fantasy wedding in Hawaii, but that's another story …

ℰ ℰ ℰ

Vickie Pokaluk

Vickie Pokaluk has over twenty years of experience traveling the garment trade centers of New York, Los Angeles, Tokyo, and Hong Kong while working for Macy's, May Company, The Broadway Stores, and Joslin's Department Stores. Her expertise is in superior customer service, satisfaction, and loyalty. She has designed and implemented organizational designs that rebuild confidence in the business, reclaim disaffected employees and customers, and deliver profit to the bottom line. Her consulting assignments have taken her from Colorado to London, Paris, and Bucharest.

Vickie's business experience enables her to relate to business audiences. Currently she is a principal, consultant, and trainer for Human Resource Asset Management Systems, Ltd. She is a member of the National Association of Female Executives, the American Society of Training and Development, the Colorado Springs Customer Service Association, and the National Speakers Association.

Vickie finds time to create a world-class garden recognized by the Miracle-Gro Company.

Vickie can be contacted at: Vickie Pokaluk
Human Resource Asset
Management Systems, Ltd.
120 Pontiac Loop
Monument, CO 80132
Colorado Springs: (719) 339-8133
Fax: (800) 472-6702
vickiepokaluk@hrams.com
www.hrams.com

So, That's What
You Think I'm Worth

By Vickie Pokaluk

Have you looked through the glass ceiling lately? What did you think you saw? Equal pay for equal work? For twenty years, I worked in retail management; in fact, my life *was* retail management. I started in high school and worked my way through college, working through training program after training program. I became a buyer for Macy's, traveling to New York, Hong Kong, and Tokyo, and spent years learning and absorbing the business. After nine years of hard work, the promotion finally came: store manager. I was responsible for 120,000 square feet, 150 employees, and a $17 million sales goal. When I walked into that store for the first time as manager, I achieved two personal career goals: to become a store manager and to make $30,000 by age thirty. (Remember, $30k was a big salary in the '70s.) Looking up at *my* store, I didn't see that glass ceiling. I saw only hope and promise and my bright future.

A few months later found me sitting in my miniature, nondescript office reviewing budgets, account by account. Then I discovered that the former manager—a man—had been making two and a half times my current salary. Same position. Same title. Same store. Except my store was doing better than ever. Wait a minute. What's going on here? Then I began to rationalize. "Oh, of course. The company was justified in paying me sooooo much less because he had more experience as a store manager. And he's older." Uhhhh, right. My argument to myself was so convincing that I continued to accept lower pay for doing the same job, even for doing a better job.

Like so many women before me and even today, the idea of challenging and negotiating salary just wasn't part of the deal. We're always so glad to be promoted that we willingly (and knowing better) accept whatever salary is offered. And of course, being women, we don't want to be seen as too aggressive.

I never mentioned this issue to the vice-president of stores, my boss. I did what women have done for so long: worked hard, developed a team, and showed increases in sales and profit throughout my first year as manager. My first performance review came, along with, "You're doing a good job," "You've built a fabulous team," "Your sales and profit are way above plan." What happened? I received a seven percent raise and a $1,500 bonus, taking my annual salary to $35,500. Still well below the previous manager, still not anywhere near parity (especially for such a glowing review). Most men at this point would have been wondering why their pay was still so low, but not me. I was too excited about my raise and still didn't question the difference with my manager. Even with no working data about other store managers' compensation, it never occurred to me to investigate.

And without that kind of comparative information, I played right into the hands of the company, willing and eager to keep any woman from breaking through.

About this time, the company engaged a major consulting firm for a compensation study on management pay, including a review of all management positions and comparing those salaries to market and salary surveys. The firm then would make a recommendation to the company addressing all levels of compensation. Upon completion of the study, our senior management held an executive meeting to share those findings and recommendations.

That meeting, held in downtown Denver on a Tuesday morning, turned out to be an unforgettable experience. All the women store managers were sitting together, as usual, and when the consulting firm reviewed their findings about store management pay, we all sat in stunned silence. Not only weren't we in the ballpark, we weren't even on the same planet. Not one of us was even at the *lowest* level of our recommended pay scale. None of the women shared their specific salaries; we were too embarrassed to talk about it. Personally, discovering that I was at least $10,000 below the beginning salary for my defined pay grade (even with my previous raises and bonuses) left me in a state of shock and disbelief. And it didn't get better. As the meeting continued, it became apparent that the company's solution to these gross inequities revolved around equity adjustments to be given over the next eighteen months. And not now, but during the subsequent review processes. So we had to hurry up and wait another year and a half to get what should have been ours all along. And of course, at that snail's pace, none of us could ever catch up. Shock and disbelief turned to frustration and anger.

I never realized the importance of gathering comparative and competitive salary information prior to taking a position. Salary was something no one discussed with one another. When I was a sales associate (my first position in retail), my first boss reprimanded me because I told my fellow employees about my first ten-cent raise. I had been so excited. She said, "You never, ever discuss salary with anyone in the workplace." That event stuck with me, even after I realized that salary secrecy was just another way to control people who needed information to stay competitive.

Returning to the store, I realized a pressing need to take charge of my career and to be compensated for the value I brought to the organization. My eyes were finally open, and I decided to resolve my salary issue. For the first time, I talked with my manager about how and when I would receive my equity adjustments. As he mumbled generalities, it was apparent that the firm had paid the consulting firm, examined the results, and promptly hoped the situation would go away.

My thought process was crystal clear. The company would give me another $4,000 or $5,000, which would pull me up—up, mind you—to entry level. And all this after being an overachieving, successful store manager for two years. But it didn't happen. Something was definitely wrong with this picture.

Now, armed with salary information, I felt it was time to look for another job. Another major retailer was entering the Denver market with three new stores and a plan for opening three more in the next three years. I had once worked for the other company's vice president of stores, so I sent her my resume. Other of my fellow women store managers also sent resumes, and we were all interviewing. (My epiphany had not occurred in a vacuum.) The company began interviewing soon after, and they called me. I knew what the position should pay, and this company was paying well within the competitive market salary range. With my newfound confidence and a solid knowledge of what I could do and what that was worth, I brought new assertiveness to discussions around job considerations, management styles, title, salary, benefits, total compensation, and my value to the organization.

My current employer found out we were interviewing, finally creating a sense of urgency toward the managers who actually ran the stores and brought in the profits. They called out the big gun: the regional human resource manager. Finally they wanted to know about expectations, aspirations, and my career. This manager told me that the company knew I was interviewing. "Why would you consider leaving us after so many years (seven), for a risky operation that would be brand new to the Denver market?" she asked. She looked me in the eye and told me I was a valued and respected store manager, and the company didn't want to lose me.

I basically told her the issue was salary—mine—and if the company valued me so much, why was I at the bottom of the salary range? Why hadn't the company addressed these inequities sooner? Why had the man I replaced made 250 percent of my salary? How much respect? How much value did they place on me?

Now I had asserted myself about my salary to two people. To close this discussion, I told the manager that if I were offered an assistant store manager job with the other company, I'd take it. Even as an assistant, my salary would be greater than my current compensation, and without all the responsibility. She followed the company line on the schedule of equity adjustments: the company would correct compensation issues over the next eighteen months.

I countered by asking how she and the company could expect any of us to wait a year and a half for compensation we could get immediately? By now, my frustration had peaked and I ended our meeting. She now knew I would leave (as would the others) and she had to do something. Because she had observed meek behavior from female managers before, she had expected timidity, acceptance, and conformance. What she got was informed, unyielding resolve.

Several of our managers left for the new company and, soon after, the company asked me to appear for a meeting with the chief financial officer. The meeting was set for a Saturday morning at the corporate offices. (That made me think, "Now they're bringing in the really big hitters, so I must be making an impression.")

So on that beautiful Saturday morning, wearing my best silk Ellen Tracy suit and looking very corporate, I found myself at the corporate headquarters office. Riding the elevator to the tenth-floor suite, I thought back to the last time I was there. Right in that office, I had accepted my store manager promotion. How things had changed in the two years since that day. Today my thoughts revolved around this meeting and its meaning to my career. I prepared myself for the standard pep talk: you're great, don't leave. I looked good, I felt good, and my confidence was high as I walked down that long, empty corridor and knocked on the chief financial officer's door.

The office. Large, oak paneling, subtly lit, and very formal. Oversized chairs, oversized desk, oversized everything. We exchanged pleasantries. Good morning. How are you? Then the pep talk began. "You're doing a great job; senior management is ecstatic over the store's performance; you've developed an exceptionally strong management team. We couldn't be more pleased with your performance." Then the other shoe dropped. "How could you consider leaving?"

In my newly found, matter-of-fact, unemotional voice, I said, "It's strictly financial. I'm extremely unhappy with my current salary, and beside myself with the proposed adjustment schedule." I noted this wasn't new information, per my previous discussions with my manager and with the regional human resource executive.

Yes, he had heard that, and he was concerned. (Not concerned enough to talk to us before we began resigning, and not concerned enough to shorten the eighteen-month compensation schedule.) He then slowly leaned forward, and with that ability that so many top executives have to be so sincere when they want to be, said in a very formal way that he had good news for me that should make me very happy.

He spoke to me as if I were a sixteen-year-old getting the car for the first time, instead of a woman who was running a seventeen million-dollar business! Effective immediately, the company was giving me a $15,000 raise, retroactive to my last review six months ago, taking me to the average ($54,000) for my pay grade. Sitting very still and not reacting, the silence spoke volumes. (Maybe he thought I was in shock.)

After what seemed like forever, he asked me what I thought about getting such a big raise. Again, no reaction on my part. I just looked him directly in the eye and remained silent. After a couple of minutes of deafening silence, I spoke without an ounce of emotion. "So, that's what you think I'm worth." We stared at one another a moment longer and I said, "Thank you for your time this morning; I really need to get back to the store." I stood up, shook his hand, thanked him again for his time, and turned and walked out that door before I lost my composure. Maybe no one—especially a woman—had ever responded to him with so little reaction, particularly in the face of a $15,000 raise. My calculated performance left him speechless.

I could barely contain myself. I was so excited that I quickly stepped into the elevator and, as it began its slow descent, I started to jump up and down, talking to myself, saying how great I was and screaming, "Yes! Yes! Yes!" Finally, finally I was where I should be: at $54,000 and the average for my job, my responsibilities, my success, my career. $54,000 still wasn't close to my predecessor's salary, but that was then and this is now. I was satisfied. In a little over two years, my starting salary had almost doubled. Most of all, for me, I didn't give management the expected, gushy "Thank you" response as I had in the past. I had earned this raise, and it was time for me to have it.

The new company didn't hire me the first go-round, so I stayed where I was for nine more months. Finally the new company offered me a store manager position. I did my research and I prepared. I made sure I received a salary reflecting my worth the way I saw it. Our negotiations produced a salary higher than the first offer, totaling a twenty-five percent increase, and finally I was where I should be. Here I was, just turning thirty-three, finally being paid what I was worth and not apologizing for it.

I learned not to go blindly into my work. I learned to research my position and to use as many sources as I could find to get as much information as I needed. I learned to negotiate and be confident of my position and my worth. I now know that the depth and breadth of this kind of information, this kind of knowledge, all translates into power. Only I and no one else could have or can take charge of my value and my worth. So in that brief conversation in the chief financial officer's office, one sentence framed the moment that I took charge of my career and life: "So, *that's what you think I'm worth.*"

Valerie A. Rawls

With close to two decades of graphic arts, marketing, and corporate communication experience, Valerie Rawls has developed a keen sense of how businesses best communicate their messages and what marketing communication vehicles deliver the best results. It is these experiences and accomplishments that led her to develop Hill Rawls Design Ink. Valerie is the founding principal and president of the award-winning marketing firm, located in Schaumburg, Illinois.

Her clients include telecommunication giants like Ameritech, ATT, and Covad; financial services clients include Computershare, MasterCard, Visa, and Wells Fargo. Other industry leading clients include Allstate, Baxter Healthcare, Commonwealth Edison, Quaker Oats, and Kraft Food Products.

She is a member of the American Marketing Association, contributes freely to select non-profit organizations, and was recently featured in the March 2002 issue of *Essence* magazine.

Valerie has special interests in several charities. Her company has provided pro bono marketing services to Horizons for Youth in Chicago, Master's Touch Ministries International in Georgia, and Urban Frontiers Mission (UFM) in Nigeria.

Valerie can be contacted at: Valerie Rawls
Hill Rawls Design Ink
420 Jason Lane
Schaumburg, IL 60173
(847) 619-5710
Fax: (847) 619-5711
vrawls@hrdi.net
www.hrdi.net

Made in His Likeness: Filling Empty Vessels

By Valerie A. Rawls

This chapter is dedicated to the memory of my father, Marshall Hill
August 2, 1934–October 13, 2000
I love you Daddy.

Give, and it shall be given unto you; good measure, pressed down, and shaken together, and running over, shall men give into your bosom. For with the same measure that ye mete withal it shall be measured to you again.
—Luke 6:38 (KJV)

Have you ever been asked, "Have you always felt the need to give, or were you taught to do it?" A local reporter was interviewing me when I was asked that question. She said, "I feel like a slacker regarding my giving commitment after hearing yours."

My response to her was that God has given each of us different gifts, and mine was to be of service to his people. According to his will and purpose our gifts vary, but they are all given from the Holy Spirit. As His "princess," that is my call, to be obedient to my heavenly father, as a child should. I also shared with her that I was blessed with a wonderful earthly father, and through his example he taught me the meaning of giving.

If I had half a penny for each time I heard, "You look just like your father, and you even have his mannerisms" while growing up, I would be a very rich woman. Being made in the image of my father and my creator became a way of life for me at a very early age. My earthly father was my living example of God's way of love. He exemplified I Corinthian chapter 13 (NIV):

If I speak in the tongues of men and of angels, but have not love, I am only a resounding gong or a clanging cymbal.

If I have the gift of prophecy and can fathom all mysteries and all knowledge, and if I have a faith that can move mountains, but have not love, I am nothing.

If I give all I possess to the poor and surrender my body to the flames, but have not love, I gain nothing.

Love is patient, love is kind. It does not envy, it does not boast, it is not proud.

It is not rude, it is not self-seeking, it is not easily angered, it keeps no record of wrongs.

Love does not delight in evil but rejoices with the truth. It always protects, always trusts, always hopes, always perseveres.

Love never fails. But where there are prophecies, they will cease; where there are tongues, they will be stilled; where there is knowledge, it will pass away.

For we know in part and we prophesy in part, but when perfection comes, the imperfect disappears.

When I was a child, I talked like a child, I thought like a child, I reasoned like a child. When I became a man, I put childish ways behind me.

Now we see but a poor reflection as in a mirror; then we shall see face to face. Now I know in part; then I shall know fully, even as I am fully known.

And now these three remain: faith, hope and love. But the greatest of these is love (NIV).

My father continued in faith, hope, and love. He had the faith to move mountains and he hoped all things, but the greatest thing to him was the love that he had for God, his family, and people. My father was a man of integrity and compassion; he truly was "a man among men."

His mantra was, "My people will be destroyed by a lack of knowledge." As a child I thought this was his observation of the state of Black America. For the majority of my childhood I had no idea these words were paraphrased from the book of Hosea, chapter 4, verse 6. The amplified Bible states it this way: "My people will be destroyed by lack of knowledge, because you [priestly nation,] have rejected knowledge, I will also reject you, that you shall be no priest to Me, seeing you have forgotten the law of your God, I will also forget your children."

His mantra became a resounding theme; it made me pursue the knowledge of God to ensure that I would not be destroyed, nor my children even though I didn't yet have any. My father wanted to see change in our community. His opinions concerning the family unit, education, and the need for economic development through business ownership were his favorite topics of discussion. The magnitude of my father's concerns regarding the lack of knowledge became my concern also. Remember, I was made in his image and after his likeness. As a "princess" and an heir to the promise, what concerned my father also concerned me.

As "daddy's girl," I was being prepared just like Esther for "such a time as this."

He was preparing me for a life of giving, by his example. Like Jesus, he was moved with compassion when he saw the needs of others. My father had a gift of discernment and he viewed people as empty vessels, himself included. He felt that it was our reasonable service to be filled and to fill those empty vessels with the knowledge given to us by the spirit of God.

Rather than continuing to just voice his concerns and opinions, he took action. He joined in the fight for civil rights in our community. He participated in discussions with the local government for equal access to public facilities. He became politically active as a precinct captain, founded a trucking company and provided employment in the community, and became one of the two first black men to join the local police force. His squad car signage read "to protect and serve," and that was truly his heart's desire.

He had charisma; I marveled at how people respected him. The Revell Bible dictionary defines "charisma" as "a gift graciously given by God, usually involving some special divine enablement for service."

I now understand that it wasn't my father others were attracted to, but a gift graciously given by God, the anointing. My earthly father was my reflection of God. By his example, I learned the principles of giving and obedience. I Corinthian 13:11 states, "When I was a child, I spake as a child, I understood as a child, I thought as a child: but when I became a man, I put away childish things" (KJV).

As a child, I participated in giving as much I could—in paper drives, food drives, walk-a-thons, and the summertime favorite, car washes for charities. But when I became an adult, I had a higher calling to give. I remember my first speaking engagement, and the audience. I was asked to speak at my high school the year that I grad-uated from college.

The purpose was to motivate and encourage the students to pursue higher education. Even though I addressed the entire student body, my presence as an African-American was an added bonus for the students of color. I was honored to be of service, and this was the first of many opportunities to speak at schools, business functions, and churches.

Giving of yourself and your talents is very rewarding. To know that you have been given the charge to assist someone as they move closer to the plan that God has for them brings an amazing sense of fulfillment. "For I know the plans I have for you," declares the Lord, "plans to prosper you and not to harm you, plans to give you hope and a future." Jeremiah 29:11 (NIV).

Several years ago, I was in the company of fifty thousand women from all over this country. We were attending a Christian women's conference that is held annually by a nationally known bishop. While in the midst of praise and worship, the Holy Spirit spoke to me regarding a certain woman who had a debt to pay who had asked the man of God to help her. The man of God had asked her, "What do you have in your house?" and she had replied, "A little oil." He told her to go and borrow all of the empty vessels and to close the door and pour the oil until all of the vessels were full. From one, many were filled.

I returned back to my home after three days of worship and fel-lowship and asked myself, "What do I have in my house to fill empty vessels with?" God gave me the answer: my talent and my business. After that revelation, he revealed to me that I would sow my gift into missions and not-for-profit organizations. I now had to be open to receive which missions and not-for-profit organizations he wanted me to give my services to.

Several weeks later I was attending a ministries and missions conference, and the speaker for the evening was a missionary Dr. Patricia Baily of Master's Touch Ministries International. She asked the question, "Did you know that there are nations on the inside of you?"

The first time I heard this my imagination took flight, and I actually saw nations on the inside of me, in my heart. The words that she spoke regarding the need for people to have a global vision for the work of the missionary and not just benevolence spoke to the innermost parts of my being. She taught about the unreached people of our world who live in a rectangular-shaped window. Also called "the Resistant Belt," the window extends from West Africa to East Asia, from ten degrees north to forty degrees north of the equator. This specific region is known as "the 10/40 Window." It is home to the majority of the world's unevangelized people. It contains only one-third of the earth's total land area, but nearly two-thirds of the world's people, with a total population nearing four billion. Of the world's fifty least evangelized countries, thirty-seven are within the 10/40 window. Those thirty-seven countries comprise ninety-five percent of the total population of the fifty least evangelized countries! Reaching these people has been her mission field for twenty years.

After the service I was given her tape series, "It's Time to Do the Stuff." A friend and sister in Christ sowed a new copy of it into my life. I enjoy giving, but I had to learn how to become a receiver. I listened to it several times for four days. On the following Sunday, the missionary was attending the morning service and our pastor asked her to briefly discuss what she had spoken about that previous Wednesday. She mentioned that she would be available to sign her new book after the service. This book was a historical view of African-American missionaries and their service in the missions' field.

Let me remind you, I now knew that I had nations on the inside of me, because I had heard the message over and over again. After the service I purchased her new book and stood in line to have it signed. While I was standing there the Holy Spirit told me to sow my business into this ministry. I placed my book in her hand and put my business card down for her to see my name. As she was reaching for my card, I said, "The Holy Spirit told me to sow my marketing communications firm into your ministry." I then asked, "Do you have a need for marketing material, a brochure, or a website?"

She started to shout, "We have been praying for you!" She called a few names and women came running to see what she was so excited about. She kept saying, "She's the one; she's the one; she's the one that God has sent; she is the answer to our prayers."

Do you know what it feels like to share the joy of someone's prayers being answered? This encounter with the missionary happened on a Sunday. That following Monday, I contacted her office. When I introduced myself, the young lady said, "I have heard about you; we thank God for your obedience to assist us."

We have to be available to God, not just as an empty vessel, but as a willing vessel. The missionary made her request: "We need a web site, and we need it in thirty days." With God, "All things are possible to him that believes." Not only did we complete the web site, we also developed a plan for the television ministry that would be broadcasting in the Middle East. What do you have in your hands? God can use it.

It's amazing that God is everywhere. Even at a computer store service counter on a Friday night. My husband and the children were out for the evening, so why didn't I take advantage of a quiet evening alone at home? Because God wanted me to meet the individual who would tell me about a young man he was mentoring and the not-for-profit organization he supported. Here we go again, another opportunity to give.

This gentleman said to me, "The people who work here look like they belong here."

My reply was, "What do you think they think we look like?"

He said, "You look like you're in advertising."

I replied, "Not bad, marketing communications." Then I told him, "You look like a bean counter," and he said, "Sales; pretty close."

God sure can strike up interesting conversations to get his job done. We exchanged business cards and he asked, "Can I have the director Audrey George-Griffin of Horizons for Youth call you this coming week?"

By now I'm sure you know what I said: "Please have her call me; I would love to talk with her." The director and I met and after I prayed about the meeting, I offered our services to her and she graciously accepted. After eight months of service, I was invited to join the board of directors. Isn't that just like God? He always works from the inside out. Each day we have an opportunity to give. As John 3:16 says, "For God so loved the world that he gave his one and only Son ... " (NIV).

Obedience and giving with a joyful heart are my "princess principles." I encourage you to ask yourself this simple question: "What do you have in your house to fill empty vessels with?" Deuteronomy 6:3 states, "Be careful to obey so that it may go well with you and that you may increase greatly in a land flowing with milk and honey, just as the Lord, the God of your fathers, promised you" (NIV).

In obedience God will bless you, so that you can be a blessing.
Give, and it shall be given unto you …
God's peace be unto you, my sisters.

Epilogue

I pray that after reading this chapter you are motivated and encouraged to begin or to continue giving. Psalm 41:11 says, "Blessed is he who has regards for the weak: the Lord delivers him in times of trouble" (NIV). We all will experience trials and tests during our lifetimes, but if we look outside of ourselves and to the needs of others in our time of troubles, we shall be delivered.

Sheryl L. Roush

Sheryl Roush conducts programs that rekindle the spirit, raise the bar, and create excitement. She relates real-life experiences in a positive, light-hearted way as she engages you, offering valuable how-to tips.

She was only the third woman in the world of Toastmasters International (in seventy-three countries) to earn their elite status of Accredited Speaker as honored for outstanding professional platform presentation skills.

Participants throughout eight countries have awarded her top ratings.

Attitude-driven communication skills topics include customer service with heart, assertiveness, interpersonal, team communication tactics, speaking/training skills, and marketing image design.

Audiences include AT&T, Intuit, Los Angeles Unified Schools, Lucent Technologies, Professional Cheerleaders, 7Up, Sheraton, Sony, Westin, and Women in Publishing Society-Hong Kong.

Sheryl is available for keynotes, workshops, and retreats.

Sheryl can be contacted at: Sheryl L. Roush
Sparkle Presentations
P.O. Box 2373
La Mesa, CA 91943
Based in San Diego, California
toll free: (800) 932-0973
(858) 569-6555
Fax: (858) 569-5924
Sheryl@SparklePresentations.com
www.SparklePresentations.com

Sparkle-Tude™!
How to Create a Sparkling
Attitude Every Day

By Sheryl L. Roush

How do you currently wake up in the morning? Is it the dog licking your face? Are the kids jumping on the bed? Or perhaps your significant other is pushing you out of bed?

How we wake up in the morning sets the *pace* for the rest of our day. And you know what kind of day it's going to be when you roll over and the dog has left you a gift—and you *step* in it!

Most of America wakes up feeling rushed—feet hitting the floor running, grabbing shoes, and heading out the door, already late for the day. We by-pass the kitchen without grabbing something nutritional for our bodies and we're out of the house. We drive in traffic, cursing every car that cuts in front of us, only to arrive late to a job we hate, slaving away for eight or more hours a day, five to seven days a week. We arrive at work, have coffee and donuts, sit at a desk in a sterile, impersonal cubicle, eat fast food for a quick thirty-minute greasy lunch, grab a candy bar and diet soda in the afternoon, and then wonder why we're so irritable, tired, or have severe mood swings.

After work, we sit back in the car and again drive home in traffic. We get home and let our loved ones know just how bad our day was, how much we hate our job, and how nothing is right in our world. That workplace negativity now enters our personal space, cherished relationships, and sanctity of home. We emotionally stuff our faces with food, plop ourselves down in front of the TV for hours, and watch non-positive programs or devastating news. Having had our fill, we head to bed, thankful that the day is finally over and that we sur-vived another one. It's more of a giving in, or giving up, than a victory!

Today, we need little attitude "boosters" to help us overcome the negative thoughts and actions that so easily creep into our daily lives. The precious princess spirit in us was born with passion, zest for life, curiosity, playfulness, and grace. Each day she exudes unbridled excite-ment, spirit, play, and candid expression—she has "Sparkle-Tude!™"

The first "Sparkle-Tude™!" booster is to start off the day on a positive tone. Perhaps you wake up to the alarm clock. What do you hear when that alarm goes off? That obnoxious buzzer? The news? A traffic report? Like that's really inspiring! (I'm still waiting for someone to create an alarm clock that, when the buzzer sounds, says, "Just *kidding!*") Perhaps you awaken to music (my personal favorite!), something a little more soothing to the soul and still effective for waking us.

Waking up a little more gently gives us a greater sense of balance, more peace of mind, and a better state of overall well being. We're equipped to face the challenges of the day and all that it may hold.

Consider waking up before the alarm goes off—with excitement for the adventures of the day!

How we wake up in the morning sets the pace for the rest of the day. I enjoy motivational music, something that jump-starts my spirit and launches me joyfully into the day with that childlike sense of wonderment and passion. Do you remember Carole King's *Tapestry* album? (Okay—do you remember *albums*?) One of my favorite songs from *Tapestry* is, "You're So Beautiful." The lyrics start out with, "You've got to get up every morning, with a smile on your face—and show the world—all the love in your heart … People gonna treat you better. You're gonna find—yes you will—you're as beautiful as you feel!"

And speaking of beautiful, the second "Sparkle-Tude™!" booster is to have only positive thoughts toward yourself and others. Guard carefully your thoughts, as our thoughts, conscious or unconscious, lead us to the Divine—the Higher Consciousness of things. Attitude, or our truest belief about things, is that highly powered magnet that either attracts—or repels! Life is composed of our moment-by-moment thoughts. The book by Napoleon Hill called *Think and Grow Rich* is all about attitude, about how we manifest prosperity and abundance by just our focused thoughts. What we conceive and believe is what we can achieve. Oprah Winfrey states, "You don't get what you deserve. You get what you *think* you deserve." And many of us need to *think* on a higher level, or more outside-of-the-box, than we have been. Start expecting great things to happen in your daily life, with limitless possibilities. Design your own destiny!

Abraham Lincoln once said, "When you look for the bad in others, you shall surely find it." The spiritual principle here is that whatever thoughts we have about other people, they are also true of ourselves, as we are all connected, and we are all one. What we see in others are reflections of ourselves. We can't see something in someone else that isn't also true about ourselves. So, believe that the opposite of Lincoln's comment is also true: When you look for the good in others, you shall surely find it. The third "Sparkle-Tude™!" booster is to look for the good in yourself and others.

Find strength in your softness. This is the fourth "Sparkle-Tude™!" booster. Believe in yourself, your talents, your unique gifts. Have authentic confidence and inner strength, regardless of what anyone else may say to you. Don't let them shape your decisions, feelings, or emotions. As #375 in *Life's Little Instruction Book* states, "Take charge of your attitude. Don't let someone else choose it for you!" The following phrase from Eleanor Roosevelt, one of the greatest First Ladies this country has ever had, gives me constant strength in dealing with others: "No one can make you feel inferior without your permission and consent."

Our attitude and choice will have everything to do with how we go through our daily lives. Earl Nightingale wrote, "Attitude is the reflection of a person and our world mirrors our attitude." Consider what these attitudes reflect …

When you think of an optimistic person, what are some of their characteristics? A positive outlook on life? They are cheerful, perhaps even wear brighter choices of clothing colors than the rest of us. And, optimists live longer lives! They have a natural tendency to look for the good in things, choosing to take the more hopeful view in life. They are assertive and sincerely care about others. They also have a personal belief system that gives them an inner strength and fortitude.

My mother is a great example of this unwavering optimism. One of seven siblings raised on a farm in Iowa, she decided very young that she wanted to create a life for herself. Consequently, at age twenty, she moved to California. She's always done whatever she put her mind to, and that's what she taught me: "You can be anything you want to be!" She always dreamed of competing in the Olympics, yet farming didn't allow her that opportunity. At age sixty-one, she carried the Olympic torch as it made its way through San Diego enroute to the Games in Los Angeles. Her full-color photo, with her smiling from ear to ear, made the front page of the local newspaper! Today she is a tour guide at the Olympic Training Center and has received the "Volunteer of the Year" award. Her "passion hobby" is working with the Olympians—getting them ready to compete. It's almost as if she lives vicariously through them. I've never seen her so happy!

Negative people, on the other hand, are like energy vampires—they suck the life right out of us even after only saying "Good Morning" to them. There are two things we can do about negative people: one, don't hang out with them, and two, don't be one of them! If you say "Hi!" or "Good Morning" to them, great! Just don't ask how their weekend was—they'll *tell* you!

The fifth "Sparkle-Tude™!" booster is not to take things "personally." If something happens during the day, without taking it "personally," observe how you are feeling and reframe the event in either a positive or neutral manner. Let it go and move on! It's not about you; it's about the situation or the event. Nothing is "good" or "bad" until we "assign it" that meaning, it just "is."

The sixth "Sparkle-Tude™!" booster is to affirm a spirit of gratitude throughout the day. I start off my day with morning affirmations. Before my feet even hit the floor, I say, "Thank you, God, for the gift of this glorious day. I rise, rejoice, and am *glad* in it. Thank you for every way in which I experience your love. I give thanks that my every thought, word, and act is only loving and supportive."

Before I speak, giving keynotes or seminars, my affirmations also include:

"Thank you for the opportunity to be of service through this presentation. I give thanks for each person present—that their needs and objectives are met, and their expectations exceeded. Thank you for their safe travel to the event. Thank you that their hearts are open to hearing this message at their highest level. Thank you for working through me. Thank you that my words flow smoothly and effortlessly. I am professional, personable, playful, and passionate. I am knowledgeable, credible, confident, and creative. I am intuitive, spontaneous, genuine, authentic, and real. Thank you that we have fun together—that we laugh and play."

After the presentation, I say, "Thank you, God, for a great presentation! That we had fun, for positive impact and inspiration. Thank you that I also grew as a result of being with this audience. Thank you for the opportunity to be of service!"

At the end of every day, I give thanks with, "Thank you, God—for this glorious day. Thank you for all the blessings this day has held (then I name them, events, people, specifics)." Consider writing in a gratitude journal (a book for only thankful things) every evening to capture those blessings and expand your awareness of your daily blessings. I fall asleep counting blessings with gratitude and awaken refreshed with a lighthearted spirit!

I have found that by starting off blessing the day—stating affirmations of what I choose to create during that day—I manifest more kindness, cooperation, and positive outcomes and feel more serenity and peace throughout the day. Is it that important? Yes! Grenville Kleiser once wrote, "Every good thought you think is contributing its share to the ultimate result of your life."

What's more, researchers in several fields of study tell us that feeling positive emotions before going to sleep builds up the immune system and wards off dis-ease and sickness. Laughing is great for building the immune system, releasing tensions, reducing stress, and lowering blood pressure. Watch something funny before you go to sleep. You'll wake up reenergized, relaxed, and happy. As an example of this, look at young children. How much would you guess the average four-year-old laughs during the course of one day? About five hundred times! They laugh at everything! Then they laugh at hearing themselves laughing! It's incredibly infectious!

How much would you guess the average *adult* laughs in one day? Not nearly as much as we ought to! Only about fifteen times a day. And even at that it's not a real laugh, but more of a grunt or a sarcastic "Ha, ha!" Yet Norman Cousins, in *Anatomy of an Illness*, says medical research shows fifteen minutes of belly-laughing has the same stress-reducing effects as six to eight hours of meditation, guided visualization, or sleep!

The seventh "Sparkle-Tude™!" booster is to have unconditional support systems:

1) Pets. They don't judge us or make rude comments (unlike some of the significant loved ones in our lives). The dog greets you at the door, wagging his tail with exuberance, instead of demanding, "Where have you been? You're four hours late!" Whenever I step out the shower, there's Tigger, my orange Tabby cat. I'm *so* glad he doesn't say, "Ahem … You're putting on a little weight there aren't you?" Pets love us. So forgiving. So supportive. They "know" when we need a hug or feel upset. Unlike some people in our lives, they don't run away at the first sign of tears! They cuddle up to us, calming us down, showing their love.

2) Faith, your personal belief system, religion, whatever that might be for you. It gives us a sense of inner strength when we believe in a power larger than ourselves.

3) Passion hobbies. These are pastimes that help us keep our sanity to do the other things we need to do in our lives. Ever

since I can remember, my father has loved organic gardening. He used to rush home after work (yes, from a job he hated), capture the daylight, and go into the "back forty" (a quarter of an acre in the backyard). I realize now that gardening is how he kept his sanity. He would take out whatever frustrations and anger he had from the day on the outside and not bring them into the house. We would lead a more balanced and centered life with these passion hobbies in our regular routines.

4) Special people. These may be relatives or people we choose to be as close as family. These are nonjudgmental, highly supportive kindred spirits. We can pick up conversations with them, right where we left off, without even missing a beat, even if it's been some time between talking. For me, Grandma Nellie, my mother's mother, is such a special person. And although she is now passed on, there's still a special place in my heart and those feelings live on. I always felt supported by her, and still do whenever I think of her and her strong Swedish spirit.

Recapture the essence of the precious princess spirit within you, the one who was born with passion, zest for life, curiosity, playfulness, and grace. Each day find ways to exude that unbridled excitement, rekindled spirit, and playfulness. Use these seven "Sparkle-Tude™!" boosters and create a sparkling attitude every day!

Attitudes are contagious—make sure yours is *worth* catching!

∾ ∾ ∾

Marilyn Sprague-Smith

*M*arilyn Sprague-Smith, M.Ed., CLL, is a catalyst for long-term positive change. She works with non-profit organizations that want to put their mission into action and with community leaders who want to create sustainable economic development. As a principal and co-founder of Miracles & Magic, Inc., Marilyn is an entrepreneurial, results-oriented consultant, professional speaker, trainer, and certified laughter leader. She consistently designs and delivers programs that harmonize group dynamics, enhance quality of work life, and produce bottom-line results. Her clients say she delivers rock-solid results in an engaging, passionate, out-of-the-box presentation style.

Marilyn is a professional member of the National Speakers Association (NSA), NSA/Carolinas, and serves on the professional advisory committee of the World Laughter Tour.

Drawing on her vast range of experiences from life inside Fortune 500 Companies to First Lady of a small rural community in western North Carolina, Marilyn weaves masterful stories that inspire her audiences to embrace the future with optimism, to change their behavior and achieve better outcomes.

Marilyn can be contacted at: Marilyn Sprague-Smith, M.Ed., CLL
Miracles & Magic, Inc.
toll free: (888) 889-6886
308 Misty Waters Lane
Jamestown, NC 27282
Marilyn@miraclesmagicinc.com
www.miraclesmagicinc.com

Dance of the D.E.E.D. Beads

By Marilyn Sprague-Smith, M.Ed., CLL

Much of my life I haven't felt good enough. When comparing myself with others, they always seemed better looking, happier, more successful than me. My attempts to feel successful, to feel good enough, seemed futile. The greater my effort, the more success seemed to play escape and evade. Nearing my mid-40s, I didn't like who I was becoming. Life wasn't any fun! I was ready for a change.

On the untamed, rugged mountain ridge the brisk, teasing breezes of early dusk delivered advance notice of the nighttime chill. The thick pallet of fallen leaves crinkled as squirrels scampered to slumber nests and nocturnal creatures began to forage for food. The leafless trees extended their bony fingers upward, beckoning the entire galaxy of stars to come out and play. The atmosphere cradled the unknown and appealed to a sense of discovery.

There we sat, perched on thick, round logs on the far side of the campfire, away from the others. Two women, engaged in let's-catch-up-conversation. Nothing heavy. Nothing intense. Just chatting.

"Barbara, how's Rodney adjusting to campus life?" I asked with casual inquiry.

"We talked yesterday. He found some new friends. He really likes his football coach," Barbara replied with genuine parental caring in her voice.

"Bet you're relieved. You were so concerned about how he'd adjust," came my feeble attempt to empathize with an offspring leaving the nest.

"He's getting settled and Garry's schedule is picking up," Barbara said as the pace of her voice accelerated. "The football schedule is heavy; we're still exploring college options. Looks like we'll be doing several campus visits soon." Barbara took a deep breath, let out a long sigh. She appeared to be juggling mentally all the to-dos.

Looking into the jumping flames of the fire, I launched a new subject. "Barbara, were you a Camp Fire Girl or a Brownie?"

A girlish smile beamed across her face as she replied, "Camp Fire Girl."

"Really! Me too!" I burst with enthusiasm, the kind that erupts from delightful surprise.

"Wo-he-lo" we said in perfect unison. We stared at each other in amazement. With "Wo-he-lo," the Camp Fire Girls' watchword, our adult conversation switched to staccato sentences, punctuated with incessant girlish giggles.

"Did you go to camp, Barbara?"

"Of c-c-c-course," she exclaimed and promptly burst into giggles.

"I didn't get to go. Every summer we had to focus on dad's passion—his garden," I said as my shoulders sagged, disappointment reflected in my eyes.

Wanting to banish the memory, I switched directions. "Did you earn lots of beads?" I asked with giddishness.

"Sort of. Bet you had tons of beads," Barbara said in coltish tone, which was so unlike her. The Barbara I knew learned new software with dogged determination.

"Ohhh, I loved those beads," I said, as a cuddly sensation swept through my body. "I'd pore over the book, looking for deeds so I could earn beads." My breath was wispy, yet filled with zest. "I earned the most beads in our group," I proclaimed and continued proudly, "I still have my jacket. How about you?"

"No." The pace was accelerating to a rapid-fire exchange, interlaced with frequent giggles. "What about your jacket? The design?"

"I designed it myself."

"Did you sew the beads on too?"

"Absolutely!"

"Really?"

"Uh huh. Sewed every one of 'em by hand. Hard to believe, isn't it? The back had strings of beads that hung to my waist. The boys liked 'em when we wore our uniforms to school on meeting day. I felt special having the most beads. You know, I really wanted that ceremonial gown. We moved the summer before I was eligible. Mom and Dad bought a business. We moved. No Camp Fire Girls. They had Brownies."

"Oh, no."

"Yeah, my jacket ended up in mom's cedar chest. She gave it to me several years ago."

Our staccato sentences and giggles caught the attention of the others. "What are you two talking about? You sound like two school-girls."

The conversation shifted. Reliving our shared experience came to a close. Adult conversation included the others. Gone were the two schoolgirls.

Hours later, off the mountain ridge and in the sanctuary of my reading room, a gnawing, restless feeling kept tugging at me. What was it about the Camp Fire Girls' experience that sparked such animated conversation?

Restlessness persisted. It nudged, "Marilyn, Marilyn, look at *me*, look at *me*!"

So I did.

I wrote on a sheet of paper, "What can I do to discover the true meaning of this experience? What is the greater message?" I got quiet. Sort of. Actually, I sat down in my recliner, closed my eyes, and took the obligatory deep breaths.

I waited … a minute.

No answer.

Thinking my request wasn't clear, I rewrote the questions in bolder handwriting. **"What can I do to discover the true meaning of this experience? What is the greater message?"**

I waited … for a few minutes.

No answer.

My hyperactive brain, now feeding on annoyance, sent a counter message. "C'mon, c'mon, c'mon. Get on with it. Get up and *do* something!"

Thinking my request needed more clarity, I rewrote the questions again, in large, bold print: **"WHAT CAN I DO TO DISCOVER**

THE TRUE MEANING OF THIS EXPERIENCE? WHAT IS THE GREATER MESSAGE?"

I waited … a few more minutes.

No answer.

My revved up, supercharged brain chattered like an agitated squirrel. "Stupid idea. Stupid idea. Stupid idea. Get up, *do* something! Get up, *do* something!"

I snapped the foot mechanism into place and sprung out of my recliner. My body projected into space like a boulder launched from a catapult. I landed, standing ramrod straight. I'd asked. I'd waited. No answer. I wanted an answer and I wanted it *now*! It was time for a conversation with the Universe.

"So, you can't speak. I've been waiting for your answer and now the line's dead. How would *you* feel if someone ignored *you*?"

Pacing back and forth across the room, my anger seared. The mental lashing went on and on. "Whose dumb idea was this 'be still and listen' stuff. Ridiculous! Nobody's home. This is a D-U-M-B idea," I declared.

Out into the world I stomped, determined to take back control. I wanted to be in charge again. I was going to figure this out myself.

Fortunately, the emotional thunderstorm subsided and a calmer, more rational, Marilyn reappeared. My anger puzzled me, yet I realized outbursts were happening more frequently. Tempestuous behavior was not going to get the result I wanted. I knew, with certainty, that it didn't work. I'd tried it for years. I needed to do something different. I knew it was important to unravel the mystery, to discover the deeper message.

The answer to my query didn't unfold for several days, nor did it reveal itself in a burst of illumination. As days passed and the answer eluded me, I did a timeline of my life. I looked for the fun things, the things that brought me joy, the times when I felt successful. And then … the answer revealed itself. As I stared at my timeline, a success pattern stared back at me. Somehow, in the years of clinging to my not-good-enough feelings, I'd refused to see it. There it was, lying dormant, waiting for me to acknowledge its presence and to use it. Also there was the ignition key. I discovered my Royal Spirit and my "Can-do Catalyst."

Unraveling the Mystery

My mother planted the first seeds of the success pattern very early in life. She nurtured a spirit of curiosity and fun, so much so that even grocery shopping was great fun. There was a prize at the end of the trip—the roll of Gold Bond or S&H Green Stamps.

At the end of each month, mother called the "lick 'em and stick 'em brigade" into active duty. My two older sisters and I gathered around the dining room table. Our job was to lick the stamps and put them in the books. This was fun because we knew we were going to trade in the books for our chosen treasures, so alluring in the premium catalogue. I wanted the treasures.

There it was on my timeline—the beginning of my success pattern. Action/reward; collect the stamps/get the treasures. I felt successful.

My timeline also revealed that Camp Fire Girls was the first opportunity to apply this action/reward formula for personal accomplishment. I wanted the beads. The success pattern was reinforced. Action/reward: do a deed, get a bead. Yet, by that time, I felt not good enough. The other girls seemed prettier, thinner, more attractive than me.

In high school the pattern was reinforced. I joined the student congress team. Our small-town team prepared to enter statewide competition against bigger, city high schools. Every team member was expected to give speeches to earn the necessary points.

On the first day of competition, the fear and trepidation of speaking before a group overwhelmed me. I had to get up and deliver my speech. The team was counting on me. We needed points. I shook, I trembled, but I gave the speech. I earned points for the team. The success pattern was reinforced. Action/reward; give the speech/get the points. Yet, again, I felt not good enough. No boys asked me to dance at the all-school dance that night.

As a high school graduate, off into the world I raced … with false bravado. I was consumed by feelings of unworthiness, of not being good enough. As I gazed at my timeline, I saw the inappropriate relationships, the career missteps, the eating disorder, the extravagant spending—my failed attempts to feel good enough. And then I saw when the pattern did an about-face.

Daring to Dream

Corporate America didn't measure up to my dreams. I decided I needed a college degree so I would be good enough.

"Do I dare risk it? Can I measure up? Am I good enough?" I questioned as my doubts plagued me.

When I met with an advisor, encouragement failed to show up. "So, you want to get your degree, while you're working fulltime," he said with skepticism. "Your goals are unrealistic. You'd better think about a seven to eight-year timeframe and that could cause some problems. Coursework is valid for only seven years," he pronounced with masculine authority.

I stared at him in disbelief. "He's an advisor," I thought. "His job is to help me plan to succeed, not to deflate my dreams."

"Here's a copy of the course requirements, the core curriculum, and the electives," he continued as he shoved a packet of paper at me. "Here's the total number of credits needed to earn a degree from this university." His fingers seemed to jab at the handout. Then, in a voice filled with superiority, he concluded, "As you can see, these are hefty requirements. You'd better rethink what you want to do, young lady."

I stared at the stapled sheets of paper. I could feel my hope for a college degree, the first in my family, slipping away. I could feel the tears welling up. A flood of *not-good-enough* emotions was ready to flow.

"Thanks for your time. I'll think about it," I muttered as I stood up abruptly, grabbed the bundle of papers, and ended the conversation. Out the door, down the stairwell, out of the building I bolted. The tears erupted.

I walked, head down, across campus to the student union. I hoped passing students weren't staring at my tear-stained face. My negative self-talk ran a ticker tape of failure messages. "I can't get a college degree. I'm not good enough. I don't fit in. I'm too fat. I have thunder thighs." It was no longer just about a college degree; I felt like a total failure.

In the student union, I managed to get a cup of coffee. I selected a table in an isolated corner. I sat and stared at the stack of papers. Tears continued their assault on my make-up. Mascara rivers streaked down my cheeks and found their way under my chin, resting in little pools until they dripped onto my once white Izod knit shirt.

My heart's desire was to earn my college degree. I didn't fit the traditional student demographics, but I *wanted* my degree! Something needed to change in the picture.

And it did.

Tears subsided. Camp Fire Girls' beads morphed into credits. "Do a deed, get a bead," danced in my head. I chose a new tune, a new beat. "Take the class, get the credits." I felt good enough!

I did earn my college degree, while working both a full-time and a part-time job. Years later, I went on to earn a Master's Degree while building a successful consulting, speaking, and training business and simultaneously serving as First Lady of a rural community in western North Carolina and being the primary caregiver for my elderly parents.

Today, I understand what helped me change the picture. It was my spirit, my Royal Spirit. I've discovered I was born with it and that it resides within. It is ever present, in all situations, at all times. I realize now that my mother taught me how my Royal Spirit works—through the D.E.E.D. self-perpetuating cycle of success:

D = Desire, having a heartfelt want

E = Enthusiasm, holding intense positive feelings towards your desire

E = Energy, doing actions that move you towards your desire; building momentum

D = Determination, holding tenaciously to your desire; overcoming all obstacles

With each accomplishment comes ever-increasing self-confidence to dare to dream. Then, you dare to dream again and the cycle repeats itself.

Knowing the Greater Message

I now know my Royal Spirit lies dormant until I ask it to help me perform a D.E.E.D. And I now understand the significance of the stamps, beads, points, and credits. They're my "Can-do Catalysts"—the counter balance to my not-good-enough self-talk. They spark my belief in self; they ignite my Royal Spirit.

Today, I reframe challenges until I find a "Can-do Catalyst" and let it be my "You can do it!" messenger. I've learned I'm worthy and can succeed when I dare to dream (desire), get excited (enthusiasm), take purposeful action (energy), and overcome the obstacles (determination).

I understand the true meaning of my mountain ridge experience. It prodded me to seek, to find, and to embrace the power of my Royal Spirit, my divine birthright

You, too, have a Royal Spirit. You, too, were born with it. You, too, have a "Can-do Catalyst." Take time to discover your "Can-do Catalyst" and let your Royal Spirit work through you. It wants to deliver your heartfelt desires. It awaits your call to action.

Indeed, I now know these three things:
I am worthy … *and so are you!*
I am regal … *and so are you!*
I am a princess … *and so are you!*

❧ ❧ ❧

Sue Stanek

Sue Stanek, Ph.D., has more than twenty years of experience supporting organizations in achieving their goals through the development of people. Sue compliments her business experience with a Master's Degree in community/adult learning and a Ph.D. in training and development.

Sue has served internally with two national healthcare organizations, Share and United Healthcare, as their training and development director. She then worked as a product manager for Wilson Learning, a leader in the field of training and development. Sue also served in the roles of sales and management for the custom training and development division of BI, a Malcom Baldrige award-winning company that provides human performance improvement systems for Fortune 500 companies.

Most recently, Sue has focused her contribution to organizations as an independent consultant of individual performance and organization development solutions. Sue partners with organizations in the areas of planning, leadership development, team building, culture development, and personal best performance.

Sue lives in Minnesota with her husband and two daughters. When not at home, you'll find her enjoying their family cabin in northern Wisconsin.

Sue can be contacted at: Sue Stanek, Ph.D.
Training and Development
Consultant
8117 W. 96th St.
Bloomington, MN 55438
(952) 943-2136
suestanek@aol.com

147

Inside-Out Applause

By Sue Stanek, Ph.D.

I impatiently filled my water bottle from the kitchen sink. If I hurried, I would only miss the beginning stretch in my favorite workout of the week. The Saturday workout meant a well-deserved post-exercise bagel, coffee, and conversation with my friends before I began my litany of errands.

As my husband appeared in our kitchen I moved around him, tossing my water bottle in my bag. I slung the bag over my shoulder and told him my schedule for the day, ending with, "So I should be back about six."

"You're running way too fast. You need to cut something out," was his response. Before I could suggest which tasks to transfer from my to-do list to his, he said, "And I am not talking about today ... I am talking about your life. You're running too fast; you're doing too much."

I looked at my husband and the clock behind him and said in a resigned-but-not-now tone, "I know … You're right … I really need to figure out a way to slow down," and moved toward the door.

His eyes, mouth, and words tightened. "You don't get it—I want you to give something up."

Confused, I said, "Today?"

Faster and louder, he said, "No—not today—today is just an example of you shoving too much into too little time. I mean give up something in your life! You are too busy—way too busy for you, let alone us."

I started to feel agitated on two levels. It looked like today's workout was a goner, and he didn't seem to get the big picture either.

In a somewhat patronizing tone, I said, "Okay … so what is it that you want me to give up? My job? (While demanding, couldn't he figure out it was paying more than his at the time?) My education? (Who could argue with the pursuit of a Ph.D.?) My volunteer work? (Could he really want me to quit my effort to create a national alcohol abuse prevention program for college students?)"

"I want you to give up the applause."

Silence.

I fell back against the wall as my workout bag and body slid to the floor. My husband's expression instantly turned from anger to compassion. His arms around me served as grounding wires while my deeply buried need, exposed in a most unexpected moment, created simultaneous tears of sadness, embarrassment, and relief. What took years to develop took only a right-time-right-place moment to unravel. That Saturday turned out to be one of the most important and difficult days in my life.

Was it an early childhood experience that created my over-active need for applause from others? Was it simply the way I was naturally wired? Did I have to give it all up to make things right? These questions and more turned over and over in my head as I took my first steps in what has turned out to be a life-long journey of balancing my strong desire for achievement and positive reinforcement from others with getting something I need from within. That something is inside-out applause. The question remains, is it natural-born need or outcome of experience?

I do think some of us are naturally drawn toward taking extraordinary measures for achievement and applause. When recently digging through my box of memories in our basement, I found my musty childhood scrapbook. I opened to a yellowed newspaper clipping titled, "Girls Win Scout Awards in Troop 81." The article reported the number of badges each of the twenty-one fourth grade Girl Scouts had earned that fall. Twenty earned between one and nine badges each. One scout earned thirteen badges. Guess who? Of course, it was me. I chuckled and shook my head, realizing I seemed to have been built for over-achievement from the get-go!

Childhood experience, too, has its place in putting this puzzle together. I grew up in a family with multiple health issues that required extraordinary attention. While we were never at a loss for love, there were times when each of us needed more nurturing and attention than circumstances allowed. Although I will never know for certain if my family situation significantly contributed to my pursuit of recognition and acknowledgement from the outside world, my hunch is that it is an important piece of my puzzle.

It is valuable for me to look at the contributing factors that have created the person I've become. I need to understand my past and then shift my attention toward creating my future. I have found I risk "victim mentality" when I put too much of my energy into the contributing reasons to my tendencies. I need to focus my energy on the more important question: "Now that I have these insights, what do I do with them?!"

As my list of insights keeps growing, so do I. I offer the following reflections on five of those insights.

Insight One: Being Busy Is Expensive!

I will likely always choose to be busy. Accepting the responsibility that goes with this trait, I need to regularly ask myself, "What am I giving up by choosing to be so busy doing what I am doing?" When I am wrapped up in the external applause type of busy-ness (which I rarely see in the moment), I can tell you what I give up:

- Connecting with my husband
- Connecting with my children
- Connecting with my friends
- Connecting with myself
- Connecting with God

These relationships pay the price—and it's expensive! We *all* miss the bond that comes with doing things together and sharing our everyday lives with each other. Yet, these relationships rarely, if ever, give me a deadline or a time requirement. Instead, they patiently wait for me to create space so we can once again connect.

This kind of awareness challenges me to change my schedule and get busy with the relationships that make my life full. What does this look like? This week it took the form of:

- Saying no to a well paying, interesting consulting job with a customer I don't like to disappoint because it conflicted with my children's summer schedule
- Taking time to make a tray of treats for my husband's fishing trip (when I gave it to him he looked very surprised and said, "Did you *make* these?" I guess it had been a while …)
- Stopping for a moment of devotion before writing this chapter

I am never too busy. I am as busy as I should be for what I have said yes to. When my life starts to feel like a whirlwind, it's simply a signal that I need to examine what I am doing and why I am doing it. The challenge is to heed the warning signals before the storm is in full swing.

Insight Two: What Am I Too Busy to Think About?

A dear friend of mine and I were enjoying lunch and updating each other on what was going on in our lives. Right in the middle of our lunch she asked me why I was so busy. As I began to explain she interrupted me and said, "Is something wrong? I know what you are doing; I just want to know why you are doing so much. Are you staying so busy that you don't have to think about something else?" I thought to myself, "Oh no, not another one of those right-time-right-moment insight-producing questions … This feels way too familiar!"

As we talked, I realized that indeed my busy-ness had its roots in seeking external appreciation to meet an internal need. I needed to, once again, balance the external and internal applause scales. With a slight smile I told her that I hate it when she holds up the what's-the-story-behind-the-story mirror. We laughed and finished our lunch. I went home, looked at my calendar, deleted what needed to go, and added what was needed to set me back on course. Although the things that needed to be changed on the schedule were difficult, a still small voice inside said, "Good job. I am pleased with you and your decision." And let me tell you, that felt better than anything had in weeks.

Insight Three: I Can Have It All!

A successful female political leader was asked, "Can you really have it all?" Her answer was, "Yes, you can. Just not at the same time." I find comfort and perspective in her words. Over time I can likely pursue and achieve all that I want. This involves patience. It can mean putting present duty before personal priorities, putting some pursuits on pause while others are realized, and letting silent affirmation of a right decision to slow down and scale back take the place of public praise of a great opportunity (but wrong timing for me) decision.

My original plan for getting my Ph.D. was to drive through it, sacrifice what was needed, and get it over with. Instead, I soul-searched, asking myself questions like the following:

- Why do I really want this degree?
- Do I really need it professionally, or is it a personal thing?
- If it's a personal thing, are my motives for external kudos or a personal sense of accomplishment?
- What is the price I pay for completing it … or not completing it?

Once I sorted out these questions, I did decide to complete it. But rather than my original plan, I took the thirteen-year route. This meant one course at a time, a five-year hiatus in the middle, and two extensions on my dissertation deadline. I did end up with the Ph.D., but not in the time frame I desired or would be proud of. The price would have been too high. I needed to let go of my need to sprint toward over-achievement and the glorious cheering I would get from the world for "doing it all" (and the world does love to cheer for that, regardless of the personal price paid). Of course, I am glad I did.

As a postscript to this story, I need to mention that no one (except others working on their Ph.D.s) has ever asked me how long it took me to get my doctorate. Why was I in such a rush? Likely, it was the lure of the applause.

Insight Four: That's Not Easy; That's Talent!

My response to a parent who profusely thanked me for taking the soccer team (seventeen thirteen-year-old girls) on a team-building retreat was, "It wasn't a big deal; anyone could have done it; I was just crazy enough to suggest it!"

When a corporate executive told me my work with her team had made a significant and sustained difference in her staff and their performance, I responded, "I am sure your follow-up was as much, or more, a part of the turn-around in your staff."

While my responses in both of the previous instances showed humility and an understanding of the bigger picture, they were also somewhat wrong. Not everyone could (or would or should!) lead a teenage soccer team team-building retreat. Not everyone could teach business people a different way of doing business, have them incorporate that learning into their work life, and see positive results.

I always assume, "Hey, if I can do it, anyone can do it!" That's not true. What comes easily to me does not come easily to everyone. What comes easily to me is in fact my God-given talent. Learning what my talents are and acknowledging them—even getting a kick out of them—creates inside-out applause.

I remind myself that it is possible to be very good at something, acknowledge it, and still be humble about it. After all, that talent was given to me. I didn't earn it or buy it. It is was a gift given to me so I could give back to the world. Now that is humbling.

Insight Five: Fan Club Friends

I have several friends who seem to always see the best in me. They're my fan club. They see the positive in everything I do. Over and over, they tell me how special I am. When I think I am doing something quite common, they point out why it is not. When I have a problem, they turn it into yet another example of my ability to face and conquer life's challenges. When I do something shortsighted or selfish, they let it instantly evaporate, or give me a quick discrete nudge to help me correct my course.

I need to continue to become that kind of friend to myself. The same applause they give me, I need to give to myself. I do that by stepping outside myself and appreciating who I am and what I do from a dear friend's perspective. The affirmations and acknowledgements I find I easily give to others, I need to find easier to give to myself. And, if not president of my own fan club, I need to at least be a member!

My Closing Curtain

Busy-ness is a means by which an important insight is revealed to me. It repeats itself as I cycle through life. When my calendar gets crazy, I can often track it back to a need to hear the roar of the crowd. I must remember that I can still have it all, but timing is important or the price will be too high. I know that appreciating my talents and using them to make a difference in our world generates joy. I need to continue to be the kind of true friend to myself that I so admire and appreciate others being to me. When I do these things I hear a different kind of applause. It takes me by surprise.

I turn around to see who's applauding and catch a reflection of myself.

◦ ◦ ◦

Amy S. Tolbert

*A*my S. Tolbert, Ph.D., develops multicultural organizations and individuals with cutting-edge topics such as fun/results-driven diversity initiatives, discovering the leader within, managing to style, and creating breakthrough teams. She is a principal of Effecting Creative Change in Organizations (ECCO International), which specializes in helping individuals expand their influence and organizations expand their global possibilities. Through e-collaboration, technology, and facilitated learning, ECCO creates a new sense of spirit and prepares people and organizations for sustainability in an ever-changing environment.

Addressing diversity and multicultural issues, Dr. Tolbert has authored "Reversing the Ostrich Approach to Diversity: Pulling Your Head Out of the Sand." She also has co-authored and presented the "Discovering Diversity Profile," a popular self-assessment tool. She has created many other electronic tools for both individual and organizational assessment.

Dr. Tolbert consults and trains in the areas of international training and development, e-learning/business television design and production, presentation/communication skills, managing diversity, and motivation and leadership. Her diverse client list includes 3M, Best Buy, Mayo Clinic, and the United Way.

Dr. Tolbert earned her Doctorate in Human Resource Development from the University of Minnesota.

Amy can be contacted at: Amy S. Tolbert, Ph.D.
ECCO International
1519 McClung Drive
St. Paul, MN 55112-1908
(651) 636-0838
Fax: (651) 636-0958
AmyTolbert@ECCOInternational.com
ECCOInternational.com

The Year of Surrender

By Amy S. Tolbert, Ph.D.

New Year's Eve

I knew my life would change that day. I was ready. I didn't know how or when, but intuitively, I knew something was about to shift. I prayed that at the strike of midnight, the heavens would open with a bolt of lightning, bless me with clear insight about my future, and turn around my trying last two years.

I was at odds with my life, being pulled in too many different directions. I was always the optimistic one, the one with the effervescent personality, but my zest waned. My business soared, but the work was not fulfilling or rewarding. My young daughters needed my constant attention. My marriage suffered. Deep inside, a great black hole was swallowing me up.

So I prayed. I prayed for a sign, a change. I should have remembered to be specific in my prayers, remembering that God has a sense of humor. Once when I prayed for a sign, it appeared the next day on

158

a marquis in big bold letters: "If you're waiting for a sign from God, this is it!" Never in my wildest dreams would I have guessed the unexpected ways God would speak to me that New Year's Eve night.

We arrived at our friends' ready to embrace the festive celebration. The temperature plummeted throughout the day and by late afternoon had dipped to just below zero. But even so, ice-skating and snowmobiling filled the day, just outside their back door, on the frozen Snake River.

Outdoor events have never been my thing, unless they involve sun, sand, and balmy weather. At dusk, the outdoor adventurers were coming in to warm themselves by the fire. I longed to stay warm by the toasty fire, too, but instead I naively opted for my first "Three Musketeers," "girls-only" snowmobile adventure. Amid the good-natured jostling about our upcoming journey, my four-year-old daughter grabbed my leg and begged me to not to go. "Mommy, it's not safe; please don't go." I gently reminded her that the others had taken turns; now it was my turn. With one tear rolling down her cheek, she pleaded, "This is different. Please, mommy, just don't go."

"How sweet," I smiled. "She's worried about her mom." I calmed her with a hug and kiss, then followed one step behind as my friends "suited up."

I rolled on the spandex facemask, leaving only a tiny window through which to see. I seated my glasses on my face and pulled the helmet over my head. Ready to go, I mounted the two-seater snowmobile sled and took a quick inventory of the controls: forward, reverse, throttle, and most importantly that day, the hand warmer. The gusty winds were whipping, pulling the wind-chill temperature down to thirty-five degrees below zero.

With a loud, deep rumble, the first snowmobile pulled out, then the second, then mine, following the gentle, sloping grade to the river.

Once we hit that wide-open space, we flew over the snow. The high-pitched motor screamed in my ears, matching the vibration I felt throughout my body.

It always seems darkest just past dusk. I tried to maintain my bearings, a task that became more difficult as the headlight bounced to and fro and my glasses steamed inside my helmet. We rode in a row of three with a breaking speed of sixty-five miles per hour. I felt like we were the great adventurers! My friends, experienced snow-mobilers, stopped for a moment in the icy darkness to check in with me. "How are you doing?" they asked.

"Great," I lied, my mind already planning a chiropractic appointment.

"Are you cold? Do you wanna go back?" they asked.

Hmmm. I hadn't noticed the bitter cold cutting through my suit until she asked. "No, I'm fine!" Another lie as I suddenly trembled. "Let's go a little farther, but we need to get back soon. We have a party to throw!"

My two friends flanked me as we started off again, like parents teaching a child to ride a bike. My breathing slowed, my heart rate calmed, and I gradually began to move with the machine. The roar of the engines interrupted the still crisp air and icy snow flew out behind us, forming great clouds as we screamed across the river.

Suddenly, I noticed there were no tracks to follow. We were in uncharted territory. The river narrowed dramatically as we shifted to single file. Through my fogged glasses, the red taillight in front grew fainter and fainter, disappearing in the fresh snow kicked-up and swirled about by the wind. I could barely make out a small wooden bridge that we would need to pass under. Then I saw it. A huge splash of water. "No," I tried to convince myself, "that can't be. We're on ice and snow. There *shouldn't* be any water here." As the words and questions whirled frantically in my mind, my body shook and tightened. The large muscles in my legs gripped the seat for security. Then I heard it. A calming, small voice I had heard before deep in my soul. My guardian angel. A clear, gentle voice commanded, "Just stop."

I reached for the brake. From behind, my friend buzzed past, crouching low in a racing position. Her engine emitted a terrifying shriek that told me she was running "wide open." I shrugged off my angel's command and did not pull the brake. But she wouldn't be denied. I heard her again, louder this time. "Stop!" As if my hand were controlled by someone else, it yanked back vigorously on the brake, causing me to fishtail and slide to an abrupt halt.

To my horror, I saw water. Lots of water inches away from me. Wide open water. My friend hung suspended in mid-air for a split second, then lost her brief fight with gravity and sank through the slush into the dark, icy water. Silence. A deafening silence. No motors, no breathing, just a stillness that seemed to go on forever.

Screams pierced the dark crisp night. I jumped off the sled and ran helplessly back and forth across the edge of the ice, pleading with my friends to tell me they were okay, shouting, "Do you have her? Is she safe?"

The light from my friend's snowmobile pointed straight to the heavens, lighting up the gently falling snow. "I have her. She's out." I finally heard. "We'll be right there. Stay still. Stop moving!"

My heart pounding, I wiped my visor to see my friends climb aboard the one sled that had made it safely across the treacherous open water. They turned and raced up the hill, over the road, and back down the other side to where I stood. They seemed to stop so far away. I wondered why. I looked down to see that I was surrounded by water on three sides, standing on a thin sheet of black ice. Panic set in. Almost as quickly, a familiar, calming voice enveloped me. My angel was with me. "Go back and sit down." A strange calm settled over me as I obeyed by gently skating a few steps and straddling the snowmobile seat once again. My friends frantically yelled to me, "Amy! The sled is too heavy! Get out of there *now*! Throw it in reverse and back out!"

I started to back up cautiously. Abruptly, I felt another hand on mine pulling the throttle back full. I turned to my right to see my friend sprinting beside the sled, trying to move us to more solid ground. We lurched awkwardly to the right, then backwards. My heart and spirits sank as a deafening crackle announced the replacement of ice by water. The motor went from a loud roar to dead silence. Again that dreaded silence …

We were in the water. I slid over the seat as the sled began to sink. It seemed to free me, while pulling my friend down with it. The silence was broken again with shrieks of "Amy! Amy, are you okay? Are you free?" She was the one trapped under the sinking sled! It struck me how she was concerned for me! She used the strong river current to pull herself out from under the heavy metal. The force of the water dragged her to the far edge of the thin ice, where our other friend lay, desperately reaching out to grab hold and pluck her out swiftly like picking a berry from a vine.

Unbelievable. She was safe. They were both safe. We were all fine, I thought. And then I realized I wasn't fine at all. I was wet. And in the water. A lot of water. Alone. The sled was sinking behind me, blocking me from my friends, and the icy water surrounded me.

My helmet visor was completely steamed up on the inside. Ice crystals formed on the outside as water splashes began to freeze. I was left in the dark. I pushed my arms out in front of me, hoping to grasp onto something … anything. In my head, the world fell silent. I bumped up against something in front of me—it was the edge of the ice. I pulled my left arm up from my shoulder and dropped it onto the ice. "That's it!" I thought. "I just need to pull myself out—that's not so hard." But my arm broke through the ice as if it were wafer-thin glass. Feverishly, I raised my right arm, then my left. It was like watching a toy run out of batteries, moving slowly and sluggishly until it stops moving altogether. I tried kicking my feet to move forward. Weighted by the freezing cold water, my heavy snowmobile suit became concrete, pulling me down. With all the flailing arm movements in and out of the water, my suit began to freeze into an icy shell.

I waited, it seemed like forever, for another command, anything from my angel. As the lights go out in a stadium, one bank at a time, I felt as if I were slipping away into darkness. I couldn't move anymore. The water began to rise above my visor, as if I were being swallowed alive. Oddly enough, the panic had left me and a peaceful sense of calm replaced it.

As I drifted slightly with the current, the silence became my friend. I began to pray softly and quietly to myself.

My peaceful moment was abruptly halted, like a needle scratching across a record. The angel's voice shook in my helmet. "You're not going to die. Just get out of the water!"

My heart responded, "I've tried everything!"

"Not everything," replied the voice softly, like it had the answer and was testing me. "What would a fish do?"

As if a movie were playing on my frozen visor, I saw fish flopping on the ice in front of me. "That's it!" I said to myself with renewed energy. I forced my arms along my side and threw my legs up behind me. The weight of the waterlogged suit sent my back and abdominals into instant spasms. Then, the tips of my boots caught on the nose of the sled. Leverage! I pushed off with my feet and threw my head back to lay my chin on the edge of the ice, wriggling back and forth, like a fish trying to get back in the water. Only I was trying desperately to get out.

Finally I was in a horizontal position, laying flat on the ice. My friends pulled me to an upright position, threw open my visor, and once again flanked me.

Smiles and gratitude quickly replaced exhaustion and disbelief. Arm in arm, we made our way to the one snowmobile still above the ice. Mounting it, however, was impossible as our suits had frozen to a solid state. For the second time that night, fear rang in the air. We realized we were too far away from the house to make it back safely with the bitter and extreme temperatures. Scanning the horizon, there were no houses nearby, and the one cell phone remaining in a waterlogged pocket was inoperable. Once again, we fell silent.

The silence broke when out of nowhere someone cried out, "Hello? Are you hurt? Is anyone still in the water?" Turning, we spotted a young couple scanning the water with dim flashlights from the top of the old bridge. We returned to the house in our rescuers' warm, safe Suburban. Loved ones flew out from every door, racing to us. As frozen snowmobile suits and clothes were peeled off, our purple and mustard tinted skin was revealed. My four-year-old wrapped her arms around my leg and looked up with tears in her eyes, pleading, "Mommy, Mommy, will you listen to me next time? Please?"

I have learned to listen. To her. To angels. To caring words of friends. Most of all, I have learned to *surrender*.

Surrender holds many secrets to the power of accepting the help of others, of being in the flow, of welcoming the unknown, of exploring deep waters … of making conscious choices.

A single stream joined by many others turns into a river with mighty force.

Many streams join, forming the powerful, majestic Snake River. We too learned to surrender ourselves, joining together to survive.

Remembering what I call "the Year of Surrender" allows me to fully accept the help of others.

Flowing water creates energy and power. When I am in the flow, inspiration, joy, and new possibilities surround me, just as I received inspiration and guidance when I let go to flow with the river current. Limiting beliefs and old habits drain energy and break life's emotional flow. "The Year of Surrender" empowers me to go with life's flow.

Wellsprings bubble up when least expected. Screaming across that river in the dark with snow billowing around us, I didn't expect to encounter water. I learned that the path to new knowledge, the path to the wellspring, often is unexpected. "The Year of Surrender" helps me welcome the unknown wellsprings.

Wonderful discoveries are made in the deep waters. The royal spirit spoke to me in the deep waters, giving me guidance when I didn't know what to do. I have learned to go deep, let go, and allow my royal spirit to work through me. "The Year of Surrender" helps me explore deep waters.

In answer to my prayers that New Year's Eve, "the Year of Surrender" taught me to reach out in faith to make conscious choices.

Crisis is a powerful way to learn, but not the only way. I was blessed in my crisis to learn to embrace a wiser slowness. Now, I take time to sparkle and dance, no longer solely fixed on my destination. I flow around obstacles and marvel in gentle currents. My newfound peace was not discovered in that icy water. It was found inside of me. With faith and surrender I welcome my royal spirit and embrace the God-given flow and course of my life. It is in surrender that true abundance abounds.

❧ ❧ ❧

Additional Resources From

Lorri Allen

Deb Gaudlin, RN, PMS

Jana L. High

Sheryl Rudd Kuhn, MRR, LMBT, CLL

Carolyn L. Larkin

Janet Luongo

Joyce C. Mills, Ph.D.

Lori Palm

Sheryl L. Rousch

Marilyn Sprague-Smith, M.Ed.

Amy S. Tolbert, Ph.D.

Additional Resources from Lorri Allen

Cassette

* *Good News! Stories True and Not So True* $10
  Original entertaining and heart-warming essays written
  and performed by Lorri. You listen and decide for yourself
  which are fiction!

CD

* *Good News! Stories True and Not So True* $15
  Original entertaining and heart-warming essays written
  and performed by Lorri. You listen and decide for yourself
  which are fiction!

Newsletters

* *Good News!*
  This is a free, monthly e-newsletter designed to uplift believers in
  their spiritual journey. To subscribe, send an e-mail to
  Lorri@Lorri.com with "GNN" in the subject line. Since its incep-
  tion in January 2000, this short message of encouragement has
  encouraged hundreds.
* *A Little Good News!*
  This is a free, monthly e-newsletter offering one tip for dealing
  with reporters and one publicity idea. To subscribe, send an e-
  mail to *Lorri@Lorri.com* with "Media Tips" in the subject line.

Ordering information:

Lorri Allen
Good News!
toll free: (888) 785-3466
www.Lorri.com

Additional Resources from Deb Gauldin, RN, PMS

Cassettes and CDs

- *Transitions*
- *Breasts with a Life of their Own*
- *PMS Blues and Other Classroom Humor—*
  Add Spice to Your Nursing Lectures
  A collection of songs about pregnancy, childbirth, and the
  adjustment to parenthood.

Videos, Cassettes, and CDs

- *It's All in the Delivery—Sheer Comic Joy*
  Live program recorded for a group of nursing students.
- *What's So Funny about Nursing School—*
  a Sure Cure for Nursing Student Blues
  Live program recorded for a group of nursing students.

Video

- *Tucked in Tight*
  A short, elegant video that sends a simple and direct message
  about aging to all in the health care and helping professions.
  Through music and images, it underscores the dignity due our
  aging population. In turn, *Tucked in Tight* invests the caregiver's
  work with dignity and purpose.

Software/Computer-Assisted Learning

- *Domestic Violence: Violence against Women*
  A multimedia program developed for healthcare organizations.

Ordering information:

To order products by Deb Gauldin, RN, *PMS*, visit her website at
www.debgauldin.com or call toll free (800) 682-2347.

Additional Resources from Jana L. High

Books

- *High-Tech Etiquette: Perfecting the Art
  of Plugged-In Politeness* $20.00
- *The Service Path: Your Roadmap
  for Building Strong Customer Loyalty!* $14.95

Cassettes & CDs

- *Tips for Powerful, Highly Effective, Dynamic Networking* $12.00
  Casette
- *High-Tech Etiquette: Perfecting the Art
  of Plugged-In Politeness.* Casette   *$12.00*
- *Stories To Make You Smile* $12.00
  An inspiring collection of Jana's most sought-after
  stories. Cassette & CD

Videos

- *How to Develop the "WOW—NOW"
  by Delivering Exceptional Customer Service* $60.00

Ordering information:

JLH PRESENTATIONS
toll free: (866) 820-6303
Fax: (972) 516-1510
jana@jlhpresentations.com
www.jlhpresentations.com

Additional Resources from
Sheryl Rudd Kuhn, MRR, LMBT, CLL

Audio Resources

- *Laughing Out Loud*
  Learn to use laughter as a stress reliever. The differences between humor and laughter explained. Learn to laugh without jokes or one liners. You'll experience an actual laughter session. Information provided on how to become a Certified Laughter Leader and/or find the closest laughter club.
- *Unhooking the Past*
  An audio version of the chapter found in this book with additional information about ceremonies and how to create your own.

Check out *www.innertouch.biz* for updates and more information on *nurturing body, honoring essence!*

Ordering information:

Sheryl Rudd Kuhn, MRR, LMBT, CLL
Writer, Massage Therapist, Speaker
Inner Touch
735 Ben Cook Road
Sylva, NC 28779
(828) 586-1761
Fax: (828) 631-3671
innertouch@earthlink.net
www.innertouch.biz

Additional Resources from Carolyn L. Larkin

Books

*   *Headlines of My Life*. Poetic conversations.
    Human Perspectives International, Inc. February 1989. $12.95

Cassettes

*   *Releasing the Compulsion to Be Perfect* (Conference). $4.95
*   *You Can't Fly with Eagles with a Bowling Ball
    in Your Mouth* (Conference). $4.95
*   *Headlines of My Life*. Poetic Conversations. $7.95

Coaching Profiles

*   *Coach for the Gold: Mining Opportunities
    for Improving Your Coaching Performance*
    Co-authored with Gary McLean and Amy Tolbert
    (to be released in August 2002)

Ordering information:

Carolyn Larkin
2669 Pala Way
Laguna Beach, CA 92651
toll free: (800) 861-3819
www.hpiintl.com

Additional Resources from Janet Luongo

Videos

* *How I Got My Paintings to Paris* $29
  Despite Stupid Bureaucrats

CDs

* *How I Got My Paintings to Paris* $19
  Despite Stupid Bureaucrats

Manuals

* *The Paris Principles of Creative Leadership Development* $44

Books

* *Mission Possible Vol. 4. How 12 Great Americans* $21
  Achieved Success (Anthology)

*Prices include shipping and handling.
CT residents, please add 6% tax.

Ordering information:

Janet Luongo
Open Minds Open Doors, LLC
toll free: (877) 307-4486
janet@openminds-opendoors.com
www.openminds-opendoors.com

Additional Resources from Joyce C. Mills, Ph.D.

Books

* *Reconnecting to the Magic of Life: Healing Stories and Practical Steppingstones—Spiritual Vitamins—for Rekindling Joy and Embracing Change*
  Quality paperback. Special offer $15.00. S & H included.
* *Therapeutic Metaphors for Children and the Child Within*
  Co-Authored with Richard J. Crowley, Ph.D.
  Winner of the 1988 Clark Vincent Award for an "outstanding contribution to the profession through a literary work."
  Quality paperback. Special offer $32.00. S & H included.
* *Little Tree: a Story for Children with Serious Medical Problems*
  A healing metaphor so powerful that its message of inspiration will be remembered long after the book is closed.
  Hardcover: $11.95 Softcover: $8.95
* *Gentle Willow: a Story for Children about Dying*
  A loving and tender tale that provides children and adults with a transformational way of viewing death and dying.
  Hardcover: $11.95 Softcover: $8.95
* *Sammy the Elephant & Mr. Camel: a Story to Help Children Overcome Bedwetting While Discovering Self-Appreciation*
  Co-Authored with Richard J. Crowley, Ph.D.
  Softcover: $8.95

Ordering information:

For endorsements, reviews, and ordering details, see website at *www.drjoycemills.com* or call 1-800-935-4770. ORDER NOW! Payable by check, money order, MasterCard, or Visa.

Additional Resources from Lori Palm

Path To Passion Activation Tools

- *Discovering Your Passion Questbook* $ 19.80
  Experiential workbook to explore the vision
  and discover your core passion.
- *Muse's Magical Wand* $ 29.70
  A power tool to create and enhance your true identity.
- *Path To Passion Pendulum* $ 22.50
  A power tool to access your intuition.
- Muse's Webweaver Kit $162.00
  Includes all three Path To Passion Activation Tools,
  plus one hour of individual consultation with Lori
  either by phone or in person.

All products are subject to tax (where applicable), shipping, and handling.

Ordering information:

Palm Productions, LLC
6033 Sumter Place North
New Hope, MN 55428
(763) 595-8223
Fax: (763) 537-3183
lori@palmproductions.com
www.palmproductions.com

Additional Resources from Sheryl L. Roush

Cassettes

• *Assertive Communication Skills for Women*	$15.00
• *Customer Service with Heart*	$15.00
• *Higher Self-Empowerment for Women*	$15.00
• *Keeping a Smile on Your Face When the Day Gets You Down*	$15.00
• *Perc-U-Lating Power: The Magic of Having More Passion & Purpose in Your Life*	$15.00
• *Solid Gold Marketing Tactics*	$9.95
Also available in CD	$14.95

Videos

• *Solid Gold One-Sheets: How to Design Speaker Promotional Materials*	$79.95

Books

• *Sparkle-Tude™: Attitude Is Everything!*	$19.95
• *Solid Gold Newsletter Design*	$24.95

Ordering information:

Sparkle Presentations
P.O. Box 2373
La Mesa, CA 91943
toll free: (800) 932-0973
(858) 569-6555
Fax: (858) 569-5924
Sheryl@SparklePresentations.com
www.SparklePresentations.com

Additional Resources from Marilyn Sprague-Smith, M.Ed., CLL

Cassettes and CDs

* *Dance of the D.E.E.D. Beads: How to Discover Your Can-Do Catalyst*
  Practical, easy-to-do tips to guide your self-discovery process.
  $15.00 cassette or CD
* *Take Time to Laugh*
  Basic tips to bring more joy and laughter into your daily living.
  $15.00 cassette or CD

Books

* *The Princess Principle: Women Helping Women Discover Their Royal Spirit.* $20.00

Comprehensive Consulting, Speaking, Training

* Consulting for Bottom-Line Success
* Speaking, Training, and Workshops
* Retreat Facilitation
* Therapeutic Laughter Sessions

Ordering information:

Miracles & Magic, Inc.
308 Misty Waters Lane
Jamestown, NC 27282
toll free: (888) 889-6886
(336) 454-8750
Fax: (336) 454-8923
Marilyn@miraclesmagicinc.com
www.miraclesmagicinc.com

Additional Resources from Amy S. Tolbert, Ph.D.

Books
- *Reversing the Ostrich Approach to Diversity: Pulling Your Head Out of the Sand.*
- *The 50 Very Best Activities for Achieving Excellent Customer Service with Special Focus on the Business & Industrial Area*

Articles (Free downloadable PDF files from website)
- "Creating the Global Learning Organization"
- "Human Capital and Diversity: Building Relationships That Affect Our Competitive Edge"
- "How to Exploit Diversity to Gain a Competitive Edge"

Instruments/Profiles/Surveys
- *Discovering Diversity Profile*
- *Coach for the Gold: Mining Opportunities for Improving Your Coaching Performance*
- *Integrating Diversity Profile*
- *CUES: Cross-Cultural Understanding and Effectiveness Survey*
- *CUES 360° Development Tool*
- *Work Environment Survey*

Education and Consulting Services
See *ECCOInternational.com*

Ordering information:
Amy S. Tolbert, Ph.D.
(651) 636-0838
ECCOInternational.com